I0830871

Mindful Parenting 101: The Art of Presence in Parenthood

Preface

Our Journey to Mindful Parenting

Parenting is a journey filled with countless joys and challenges, but for us, it has been a journey marked by resilience and perseverance in the face of serious health battles. We, Jawahar Soundararajan and Karthik Raghuraman, have each faced life-threatening illnesses in our early 30s that forever changed our perspectives on life and parenting.

I, Jawahar, battled lymphoma not once but twice. The diagnosis was a shock, but with the support of my family and the strength I found within myself, I survived the grueling treatment. Today, I live in Michigan with my wife and our two beautiful daughters, working as a software architect. The experience taught me the importance of being present, of cherishing each moment with my family, and of raising my children with mindfulness and intention.

Karthik's journey was equally challenging. Diagnosed with Crohn's disease in his early 30s, he faced years of pain, uncertainty, and intensive treatment. But through it all, Karthik remained focused on his family and his career. Now living in New Jersey with his wife and two sons, and working as a Digital Learning Lead, he has used his experience to embrace a mindful approach to parenting—one that prioritizes emotional connection and resilience in the face of life's unpredictability.

Why We Wrote This Book

This book, "Mindful Parenting 101: Cultivating Presence in Parenthood," is born out of our real-life experiences as fathers who have navigated the dual challenges of serious illness and raising a family. We've learned, often the hard way, that mindfulness is not just a concept but a vital practice that has helped us stay grounded and connected with our children, even during the most difficult times.

Our experiences have taught us that life's toughest moments can also be the most transformative. Through mindfulness, we found a way to remain present for our families, to guide our children with compassion, and to maintain our own emotional and mental well-being.

The Role of AI in Our Writing Process

While this book draws deeply from our personal journeys and the lessons we've learned along the way, we also harnessed the power of artificial intelligence to help us research and organize our thoughts. AI was a valuable tool in gathering insights and structuring the content, but every word has been carefully reviewed, edited, and refined by us to ensure that it reflects our experiences and our vision for this book.

A Personal Invitation

We invite you to join us on this journey toward more mindful parenting. Whether you are dealing with your own life challenges or simply seeking to be more present with your children, we hope that the strategies and insights in this book will provide you with the tools and inspiration you need. This book is a testament to the resilience of the human spirit and the power of mindfulness in navigating the complexities of parenthood.

Acknowledgments

We want to express our deepest gratitude to our families, who have been our pillars of strength through our health battles and beyond. Their love and support have been the foundation of everything we do. We also thank the technology that assisted us in bringing this book to life, allowing us to share our story and our insights with you.

Disclaimer

This book has been created with the assistance of artificial intelligence (AI). The content, including the structure, examples, and guidance, has been developed through a collaborative effort between human authors and AI technology. While AI has provided support in generating and organizing the material, all content has been carefully reviewed, edited, and refined by the authors to ensure accuracy, relevance, and quality.

The information in this book is intended to provide general guidance on mindful parenting. It is not a substitute for professional advice, and readers are encouraged to consult relevant experts or professionals for specific concerns or situations.

The authors and publishers are not liable for any outcomes resulting from the application of the concepts or practices described in this book.

Mindful Parenting 101: The Art of Presence in Parenthood

Introduction

Parenting is one of life's most rewarding and challenging journeys. It's a path filled with joy, love, and fulfillment, but also one that brings stress, uncertainty, and moments of self-doubt. Imagine the first time you held your newborn, feeling an overwhelming surge of love and responsibility. Or think about the late-night moments when your child is sick, and you're torn between comforting them and managing your own exhaustion. These moments encapsulate the beauty and complexity of parenthood.

In the hustle and bustle of daily life, it's easy to find ourselves caught in a whirlwind of responsibilities—rushing from one task to the next, trying to balance work, household chores, and our children's needs. Picture a typical morning: preparing breakfast, getting everyone dressed, managing school drop-offs, and juggling work deadlines—all before the clock even hits noon. In the midst of this chaos, we can sometimes lose sight of what truly matters: being present with our children.

Mindful parenting offers a way to reconnect with the essence of parenthood. It's about slowing down, tuning into the present moment, and cultivating a deeper awareness of both ourselves and our children. For instance, instead of reacting to your child's tantrum with frustration, mindful parenting encourages you to pause, take a deep breath, and approach the situation with empathy and understanding. Mindfulness in parenting isn't about striving for perfection or following a rigid set of rules. Instead, it's about embracing each moment with our children—whether joyful, challenging, or mundane—with an open heart and a calm mind.

At its core, mindful parenting is about presence. It's about being fully engaged in the here and now, free from distractions and judgments. When we parent mindfully, we create a space of love and safety where our children can thrive. Imagine sitting down for dinner with your family, fully engaged in conversation without the distraction of phones or TV. We listen more deeply, respond more thoughtfully, and connect more meaningfully. We also model for our children how to navigate life's ups and downs with grace and resilience.

This book is an invitation to explore what it means to be a mindful parent. Throughout these pages, we will delve into practical strategies, reflective exercises, and gentle guidance to help you bring more mindfulness into your parenting journey. You'll learn how to manage your own stress and emotions, communicate with your child in a way that fosters connection, and create a home environment that nurtures both you and your child.

Consider Sarah, a mother of two who felt overwhelmed by the constant demands of her family. By incorporating mindfulness practices, she found moments of calm in her daily routine, improved her patience, and strengthened her bond with her children. Her story is one of many that illustrate the transformative power of mindful parenting.

Whether you're a new parent or have been on this journey for many years, this book is here to support you. Mindful parenting is not about doing more, but about being more—more present, more aware, and more connected with your child. It's about finding moments of calm in the midst of the storm and bringing a sense of peace and intention to your everyday interactions.

As you begin this journey into mindful parenting, remember to be kind to yourself. Parenting is not always easy, and there will be moments when you fall short of your own expectations. That's okay. Mindfulness teaches us to accept each moment as it is, with compassion and without judgment. Every moment is an opportunity to start anew, to connect more deeply with your child, and to grow together.

So, let's embark on this journey of mindful parenting together. Let's explore how we can cultivate presence, deepen our connections, and create a nurturing environment where both we and our children can flourish. Welcome to the art of mindful parenting.

Chapter 1: The Foundation of Mindfulness

Parenting is a journey filled with love, joy, and countless challenges. It's a path that requires patience, understanding, and the ability to adapt to ever-changing situations. But at the heart of this journey is one simple yet profound principle: presence. Being truly present with your child, in the here and now, is the essence of mindful parenting.

Understanding Mindfulness

Mindfulness is more than just a buzzword or a trendy concept. It's a way of living that encourages us to pay attention to the present moment, with curiosity and without judgment. It's about noticing what's happening right now—both within ourselves and in the world around us—and responding with intention rather than reacting on autopilot.

Imagine a morning where everything seems to be going wrong. You're running late, your child is refusing to get dressed, and the stress is mounting with each passing minute. It's easy to let frustration take over, leading to a rushed, tense exchange that leaves both you and your child feeling upset. But now imagine the same scenario with a mindful approach. As the stress begins to build, you take a deep breath, grounding yourself in the present moment. You notice the tightness in your chest, the hurried thoughts in your mind, and you consciously choose to respond differently. Instead of snapping at your child, you kneel down, look into their eyes, and gently say, "I know getting dressed can be hard sometimes. How about we do it together?" This small shift in approach transforms the moment, turning a potential conflict into an opportunity for connection.

The Role of Self-Awareness in Parenting

At the core of mindfulness is self-awareness—the ability to recognize and understand your own emotions, thoughts, and behaviors. In the context of parenting, self-awareness is crucial. It helps you identify when you're being triggered, why you're reacting in a certain way, and how you can choose a more mindful response.

Let's consider the story of Claire, a mother of two young children. Claire often found herself losing patience during the hectic dinner hour. By the time she'd cooked, served the meal, and sat down, her nerves were already frayed. When her children started to squabble or refuse to eat, she would quickly snap, raising her voice and sending them to their rooms. Afterward, she would feel guilty and frustrated, wondering why she couldn't stay calm. One evening, Claire decided to try something different. She took a few minutes before dinner to sit quietly and breathe, noticing the tension in her body and the worries in her mind. She recognized that her impatience was often fueled by her own exhaustion and unmet needs. Armed with this awareness, Claire approached dinner with a different mindset. When her children began to argue, she paused, took a deep breath, and calmly addressed the situation. "I can see you're both upset," she said, "Let's talk about what's bothering you after we finish eating." This small change in her approach led to a more peaceful dinner and left Claire feeling more in control and less reactive.

Self-awareness allows you to step back from automatic reactions and choose how you want to respond to your child. It's not about suppressing your emotions or pretending everything is fine when it's not. Instead, it's about acknowledging what you're feeling, understanding where those feelings are coming from, and deciding how to respond in a way that aligns with your values as a parent.

Building Emotional Intelligence

Emotional intelligence is the ability to recognize, understand, and manage your own emotions, as well as the emotions of others. It's a key component of mindful parenting because it helps you navigate the emotional landscape of family life with empathy and resilience.

Take the example of Sarah, a mother who often felt overwhelmed by her son's emotional outbursts. Whenever he became upset, Sarah would try to fix the problem quickly, offering solutions or telling him to calm down. But this approach often backfired, leaving her son feeling unheard and Sarah feeling frustrated. After learning about emotional intelligence, Sarah decided to try a new approach. The next time her son had a meltdown, she sat with him, placing a gentle hand on his shoulder, and simply said, "I'm here with you. It's okay to feel upset." She didn't try to solve the problem right away; instead, she listened to him and acknowledged his feelings. As her son began to calm down, Sarah asked him if he wanted to talk about what was bothering him. This simple act of empathy and presence made a significant difference. Her son felt understood, and they were able to work through the issue together.

Building emotional intelligence in yourself and your child creates a foundation for a strong, healthy relationship. It teaches your child that all emotions are valid and that they can be managed in a constructive way. It also helps you stay calm and connected, even in the midst of challenging situations.

Practical Exercises for Mindful Parenting

Here are some simple exercises you can incorporate into your daily life to build mindfulness and self-awareness in your parenting:

1. **Mindful Check-In:**
   - **How to do it:** Set aside a few moments each day to check in with yourself. Close your eyes, take a deep breath, and notice how you're feeling—physically, emotionally, and mentally. Acknowledge whatever comes up without judgment. This practice helps you become more aware of your internal state and prepares you to respond mindfully throughout the day.
   - **Example:** Before picking up your child from school, take a minute to check in with yourself. Notice if you're feeling rushed, stressed, or tired, and take a few deep breaths to center yourself. This will help you greet your child with a calm, open presence.
2. **Three Deep Breaths:**
   - **How to do it:** Whenever you feel yourself getting triggered or overwhelmed, pause and take three deep breaths. Inhale slowly through your nose, hold for a count of three, and exhale slowly through your mouth. This simple practice can help you calm your nervous system and create space for a more mindful response.

- o **Example:** If your child starts to argue with a sibling, and you feel your frustration rising, use this technique before responding. The brief pause can make a significant difference in how you handle the situation.

3. **Gratitude Practice:**
   - o **How to do it:** At the end of each day, take a moment to reflect on three things you're grateful for. These can be small moments of connection with your child, acts of kindness, or anything that brought you joy during the day. Gratitude shifts your focus from what's stressful or challenging to what's positive and uplifting.
   - o **Example:** After a long day, instead of focusing on the challenges, take a moment to remember the smile your child gave you when you read their favorite bedtime story or the way they thanked you for helping with a difficult task. This practice not only lifts your mood but also helps you approach the next day with a more positive mindset.

4. **Mindful Listening:**
   - o **How to do it:** The next time your child talks to you, practice mindful listening. Give them your full attention, make eye contact, and really listen to what they're saying without interrupting or planning your response. Reflect back what you hear to show that you understand.
   - o **Example:** When your child comes home from school and starts talking about their day, put aside what you're doing, and listen fully. Reflect back by saying something like, "It sounds like you had a really exciting day," or "I can see why that was

frustrating for you." This simple act of mindful listening can deepen your connection and make your child feel truly heard.

5. **Body Scan Meditation:**
   - **How to do it:** This exercise helps you become more aware of your physical state and release tension. Sit or lie down in a comfortable position, and slowly bring your attention to different parts of your body, starting from your toes and moving up to your head. Notice any sensations, areas of tension, or discomfort, and breathe into those areas, releasing tension with each exhale.
   - **Example:** After a stressful day, take five minutes to do a body scan before bed. This practice can help you release the physical tension you've accumulated throughout the day, making it easier to rest and recharge for the next day.

By integrating mindfulness into your daily life, you create a strong foundation for a more present, connected, and compassionate approach to parenting. Remember that mindfulness is a practice—it's not about being perfect but about making small, intentional choices each day that bring you closer to the parent you want to be.

As you move forward on this journey, be patient with yourself. There will be moments of frustration and moments of joy, and each one is an opportunity to learn, grow, and deepen your connection with your child. Mindful parenting is not a destination but a continuous process of becoming more aware, more compassionate, and more present in the beautiful, messy, and ever-changing adventure of raising a child.

Chapter 2: Building Emotional Intelligence

Parenting is an emotional journey. From the joy of your child's first smile to the frustration of sleepless nights, emotions run high on this path. Navigating these emotions—both yours and your child's—is essential to creating a harmonious and supportive environment at home. This is where emotional intelligence comes into play. Emotional intelligence is the ability to recognize, understand, and manage your own emotions, as well as to recognize and influence the emotions of others. It's a skill that lies at the heart of mindful parenting and is crucial for fostering deep, healthy relationships with your child.

Recognizing and Managing Your Emotions

As a parent, you experience a wide range of emotions on any given day—love, joy, pride, but also frustration, anger, and anxiety. These emotions are natural and valid, but how you manage them can make all the difference in your interactions with your child. Developing emotional intelligence starts with recognizing your own emotions, understanding their origins, and learning to manage them in a way that aligns with your values as a parent.

Scenario: The Power of Self-Awareness

Consider the story of Emma, a mother of two young children. One afternoon, after a long and stressful day at work, Emma came home to find her living room in chaos—her children had scattered toys everywhere, and her youngest was having a meltdown over a broken crayon. Exhausted and overwhelmed, Emma felt a surge of irritation and anger bubbling up inside her. In the past, she might have reacted by snapping at her children, raising her voice, and demanding that they clean up immediately. But Emma had been working on her emotional intelligence, and she decided to try something different.

Emma paused for a moment, taking a deep breath and noticing the tightness in her chest and the heat in her face—signs of her rising anger. She acknowledged her feelings internally, recognizing that her frustration wasn't just about the mess or the meltdown; it was also about her own fatigue and the stress she had brought home from work. With this awareness, Emma chose to respond differently. Instead of yelling, she walked over to her youngest, knelt down to his level, and gently asked, "I can see you're really upset. Do you want to tell me what happened?" Her calm and empathetic approach helped her child feel heard and soothed, and together they began to clean up the mess. By managing her own emotions, Emma was able to defuse the situation and create a more positive outcome for everyone involved.

Techniques for Managing Your Emotions

Learning to manage your emotions doesn't mean suppressing them or pretending they don't exist. It's about recognizing what you're feeling, understanding why you're feeling that way, and choosing how to respond in a way that's consistent with your goals as a parent.

1. **The Pause Button:**
    - **How to do it:** When you feel a strong emotion rising—whether it's anger, frustration, or anxiety—pause before reacting. Take a deep breath, count

to three, and give yourself a moment to think before you respond.

- o **Example:** Imagine you're in the middle of a tense conversation with your teenager, and you feel your temper rising. Instead of snapping back, you take a deep breath and pause. This brief moment of reflection helps you respond calmly and constructively, rather than escalating the conflict.

2. **Label Your Emotions:**
   - o **How to do it:** When you notice a strong emotion, name it. Say to yourself, "I'm feeling angry," or "I'm feeling anxious." Labeling your emotions can help you gain a clearer understanding of what you're experiencing and reduce the intensity of the feeling.
   - o **Example:** When Sarah's toddler threw a tantrum at the grocery store, she felt overwhelmed by embarrassment and frustration. Instead of reacting immediately, she silently named her emotions: "I'm feeling embarrassed because people are watching, and I'm frustrated because I don't know how to calm him down." This simple act of labeling helped Sarah gain clarity and approach the situation more calmly.

3. **Practice Deep Breathing:**
   - o **How to do it:** Deep breathing is a powerful tool for calming the nervous system. When you feel overwhelmed, take a few deep breaths, inhaling slowly through your nose and exhaling through your mouth. Focus on the sensation of the breath entering and leaving your body.

- o **Example:** During a particularly chaotic morning, when everything seemed to be going wrong, Jessica felt her stress levels skyrocketing. Instead of letting the stress take over, she stepped into another room, closed her eyes, and took several deep breaths. As she focused on her breathing, she felt her body begin to relax, and she returned to her family with a renewed sense of calm.

4. **Use Positive Self-Talk:**
   - o **How to do it:** Replace negative thoughts with positive affirmations. Instead of thinking, "I can't handle this," remind yourself, "I'm doing the best I can," or "I have the strength to get through this."
   - o **Example:** After a long day, when Mark's three-year-old refused to go to bed, he felt his frustration growing. His initial thought was, "Why won't she just go to sleep? I can't deal with this right now." But Mark consciously replaced this thought with, "I'm tired, but I can handle this. We'll get through bedtime together." This shift in mindset helped him approach the situation with more patience and compassion.

5. **Mindful Reflection:**
   - o **How to do it:** After a difficult moment with your child, take time to reflect on what happened. Ask yourself what emotions were present, how you reacted, and what you might do differently next time. This reflection helps build emotional awareness and prepares you for future challenges.
   - o **Example:** After a heated argument with her teenager about curfew, Rachel felt a mix of anger, guilt, and sadness. Later that evening, she spent

some time journaling about the argument—what triggered her emotions, how she responded, and what she could have done differently. Through this reflection, Rachel gained insight into her own triggers and resolved to approach future conflicts with more understanding.

Helping Your Child Navigate Their Emotions

Just as it's important for parents to manage their own emotions, it's equally vital to guide children in understanding and managing theirs. Children, especially young ones, are still learning how to identify and express their emotions. As a parent, you can play a crucial role in helping them develop emotional intelligence by modeling emotional regulation and providing a safe space for them to express their feelings.

Scenario: Teaching Emotional Intelligence Through Play

Let's consider the story of Lucas, a five-year-old who often became frustrated when he couldn't solve a puzzle. His immediate response was to cry and push the puzzle away, saying, "I can't do it!" His mother, Amy, saw this as an opportunity to teach Lucas about emotional intelligence. Instead of simply telling him to calm down or try again, Amy sat down with Lucas and helped him identify his emotions. "I see you're feeling frustrated because the puzzle is really hard," she said. "It's okay to feel frustrated. Do you want to take a deep breath with me and try one more time?" They practiced taking deep breaths together, and then Amy encouraged Lucas to approach the puzzle again, this time with a calmer mind. Over time, Lucas learned to recognize his frustration, take a breath, and persevere through challenges—a skill that would serve him well beyond the world of puzzles.

Techniques for Supporting Your Child's Emotional Development

1. **Teach Emotional Vocabulary:**
   - **How to do it:** Help your child learn to identify and name their emotions. Use everyday situations to teach them words for their feelings—happy, sad, frustrated, excited, etc. This empowers them to express themselves clearly and reduces frustration.
   - **Example:** When Lily was upset because she couldn't have a second cookie, her mother, Karen, said, "I can see you're feeling disappointed because you really wanted another cookie." By naming the emotion, Karen helped Lily understand and articulate what she was feeling.
2. **Acknowledge Their Feelings:**
   - **How to do it:** Validating your child's emotions shows that you understand and accept what they're experiencing, even if you don't agree with the behavior. This builds trust and helps them feel safe expressing themselves.
   - **Example:** When Jack, a seven-year-old, was angry because his friend didn't share a toy, his father, Tom, said, "I understand that you're angry. It's hard when someone doesn't share with you." Tom didn't dismiss Jack's feelings but instead acknowledged them, helping Jack feel understood.
3. **Model Emotional Regulation:**

- **How to do it:** Children learn a lot by observing their parents. By managing your own emotions in healthy ways, you model for your child how to handle their feelings. This might mean taking deep breaths when you're stressed or calmly talking about your feelings.
- **Example:** During a family game night, when things got competitive and her son, Max, started to get upset, Laura modeled taking a deep breath and said, "I'm feeling a little frustrated too, so I'm going to take a deep breath to calm down." Max watched his mother, mimicked her behavior, and gradually learned to regulate his own emotions in a similar way.

4. **Create a Safe Space for Expression:**
   - **How to do it:** Encourage your child to express their emotions in a healthy way, whether through talking, drawing, or even physical activity. Let them know that all feelings are okay, but it's how we express them that matters.
   - **Example:** After a challenging day at school, Emily's daughter, Sophie, came home feeling angry and upset. Instead of telling Sophie to calm down immediately, Emily offered her some paper and crayons and said, "Why don't you draw how you're feeling?" This gave Sophie an outlet for her emotions and helped her process her feelings in a constructive way.

5. **Guide Problem-Solving:**
   - **How to do it:** When your child is upset, help them find constructive solutions to their problems. Instead of solving the problem for them, guide

them through the process of identifying their feelings, understanding the situation, and brainstorming solutions.

- o **Example:** When nine-year-old Ben was upset about a disagreement with his friend, his mother, Jessica, didn't jump in with advice. Instead, she asked, "How did that make you feel? What do you think you could do to make things better?" Together, they talked through the situation, and Ben came up with a plan to talk to his friend the next day. This approach empowered Ben to handle the situation with confidence and taught him valuable problem-solving skills.

Building emotional intelligence—both in yourself and in your child—is a foundational aspect of mindful parenting. It's about creating an environment where emotions are recognized, understood, and managed in a healthy way. By developing these skills, you not only strengthen your relationship with your child but also equip them with the tools they need to navigate the emotional complexities of life. As you continue on this journey, remember that emotional intelligence is not a destination but a practice. Each day brings new opportunities to learn, grow, and deepen your connection with your child through the power of emotional awareness and mindfulness.

Chapter 3: Mindful Communication

Active Listening and Empathy

Communication is the bridge that connects us with our children, but all too often, it's a bridge that is underused or misused. How many times have you half-listened to your child while distracted by your phone, or rushed through their stories because you were preoccupied with other tasks? Mindful communication is about being fully present in your interactions with your child, ensuring that they feel heard, understood, and valued.

The Importance of Active Listening

Listening is more than just hearing the words your child is saying; it's about truly understanding the message they're trying to convey, both verbally and non-verbally. Active listening involves giving your full attention, being aware of your child's emotions, and reflecting back what you hear to show that you understand.

Scenario: The Power of Presence

Consider the story of Liam, a busy father of two. After a long day at work, Liam would often come home, only to find himself distracted by his phone or his thoughts as his seven-year-old daughter, Ella, tried to tell him about her day. He would nod and say "uh-huh" while checking emails, not fully engaged in the conversation. Over time, Ella began to share less with her father, sensing that he wasn't truly listening. One evening, Liam noticed this change and realized that his distracted listening was affecting their relationship. Determined to reconnect, he decided to make a change.

The next day, when Ella started talking about her day at school, Liam put down his phone, made eye contact, and gave her his full attention. He listened intently, asked open-ended questions, and reflected back what she said to show that he was engaged. "That sounds like a really fun art project, Ella! How did you come up with the idea for your painting?" Ella's face lit up, and she eagerly continued the conversation, feeling valued and understood. Liam's simple act of mindful listening strengthened their connection, making Ella feel more comfortable and confident in sharing her thoughts and feelings.

Practices for Enhancing Active Listening

1. **Give Your Full Attention:**
   - **How to do it:** When your child is speaking, put aside any distractions, whether it's your phone, a book, or a task you're working on. Make eye contact, lean in slightly, and show through your body language that you're fully present.
   - **Example:** If your teenager comes to you to talk about something that's bothering them, resist the urge to continue folding laundry or checking your phone. Sit down with them, face them directly, and listen attentively. Your full attention communicates that what they're saying is important to you.
2. **Reflect Back What You Hear:**
   - **How to do it:** After your child speaks, reflect back what you heard to show that you understand. This could be summarizing what they said or repeating

a key point in your own words. This practice not only shows that you're listening but also helps your child clarify their own thoughts.

- ○ **Example:** When your child says, "I'm really upset because my friend didn't play with me at recess," you might respond with, "It sounds like you felt left out and that really hurt your feelings." Reflecting back their words helps them feel understood and validates their emotions.

3. **Ask Open-Ended Questions:**
   - ○ **How to do it:** Encourage your child to share more by asking open-ended questions—those that can't be answered with just a "yes" or "no." This invites them to express their thoughts and feelings more fully.
   - ○ **Example:** Instead of asking, "Did you have a good day at school?" try asking, "What was the most interesting thing that happened at school today?" This type of question encourages your child to think more deeply and share more about their experiences.

4. **Be Patient and Don't Interrupt:**
   - ○ **How to do it:** Give your child the time they need to express themselves without interrupting or finishing their sentences. Patience in listening shows respect for their thoughts and feelings.
   - ○ **Example:** If your young child is struggling to explain a problem they had at school, allow them to take their time. Resist the urge to jump in with solutions or assumptions. Your patience helps them feel safe and supported in sharing their thoughts.

5. **Acknowledge Non-Verbal Cues:**

- o **How to do it:** Pay attention to your child's body language, facial expressions, and tone of voice. These non-verbal cues often convey more than the words themselves. Acknowledge what you notice to deepen your understanding.
- o **Example:** If your child comes home with a frown and slumps into a chair, you might say, "I can see that something's bothering you. Do you want to talk about it?" Recognizing and addressing their non-verbal cues shows that you're attuned to their emotional state.

Communicating with Empathy

Empathy is the ability to understand and share the feelings of another person. In mindful parenting, communicating with empathy means putting yourself in your child's shoes, seeing the world from their perspective, and responding with kindness and understanding.

Scenario: Empathy in Action

Emma, a mother of a teenage son named Jake, often found herself frustrated by his apparent lack of interest in spending time with the family. Jake would retreat to his room after school, barely speaking a word during dinner, and would often seem distant and moody. Emma's initial reaction was to feel hurt and rejected, interpreting Jake's behavior as a sign that he didn't care about the family. But one evening, after reading about the challenges of adolescence, Emma decided to approach the situation with empathy.

Instead of confronting Jake about his behavior, Emma quietly knocked on his door and asked if she could sit with him for a while. She didn't press him with questions or demand that he join the family downstairs. Instead, she simply said, "I know being a teenager can be really tough sometimes. I just want you to know that I'm here if you ever want to talk, or if you just need some company." Jake didn't say much at first, but over the next few days, he began to open up bit by bit. He shared that he'd been feeling overwhelmed by school and friendships, and that he retreated to his room to cope. By approaching Jake with empathy, Emma created a safe space for him to share his struggles, deepening their connection and helping him feel understood.

Practices for Cultivating Empathy in Communication

1. **Put Yourself in Their Shoes:**
   - **How to do it:** When your child is expressing a difficult emotion, take a moment to imagine how they must be feeling. Consider what might be going through their mind and how you would feel in their situation. This perspective shift can help you respond with greater compassion.
   - **Example:** If your child is angry because they weren't invited to a friend's birthday party, instead of dismissing their feelings, you might say, "I can see why you're upset. It really hurts to feel left out." This empathetic response shows that you understand and respect their emotions.
2. **Validate Their Feelings:**
   - **How to do it:** Even if you don't fully understand why your child feels a certain way, it's important to acknowledge that their feelings are real and valid.

This doesn't mean you have to agree with their perspective, but it does mean recognizing their emotional experience.

- o **Example:** When your teenager slams the door after an argument, you might feel frustrated by their reaction. But instead of responding with anger, you might knock on their door later and say, "I know you were really upset earlier, and that's okay. Let's talk about it when you're ready." This validation helps them feel seen and respected.

3. **Use Empathetic Language:**
   - o **How to do it:** Use language that expresses empathy and understanding. Phrases like, "I hear you," "That sounds really tough," or "I'm here for you" can go a long way in showing your child that you're on their side.
   - o **Example:** After a difficult day at school, your child might express frustration by saying, "I hate school, and I'm never going back!" Instead of dismissing this outburst, you could respond with, "It sounds like today was really hard for you. I'm sorry you're feeling this way. Do you want to talk about what happened?" This empathetic language opens the door for deeper communication.

4. **Practice Compassionate Responses:**
   - o **How to do it:** When your child makes a mistake or behaves in a way that frustrates you, try to respond with compassion rather than criticism. Remember that they are still learning and growing, just like you.
   - o **Example:** When your child accidentally breaks a glass while helping with the dishes, instead of

scolding them, you might say, "I know you didn't mean to break it. Let's clean it up together." This compassionate response teaches them that it's okay to make mistakes and that they can learn from them without fear of harsh judgment.

5. **Show Understanding Through Actions:**
   - **How to do it:** Sometimes, showing empathy goes beyond words. It's about being there for your child in ways that matter to them—whether it's sitting quietly with them when they're upset, offering a hug, or simply being present without needing to "fix" anything.
   - **Example:** After a tough day, your child might not want to talk but just wants to sit with you while watching a movie or reading a book. By simply being there with them, you show that you understand their need for comfort and connection without forcing them to talk about what's bothering them.

Mindful Conflict Resolution

Conflict is a natural part of any relationship, including the parent-child dynamic. Whether it's a disagreement over bedtime, homework, or household chores, conflicts provide an opportunity to practice mindful communication and teach your child valuable skills for resolving disagreements peacefully.

Scenario: Navigating Conflict with Mindfulness

During a particularly stressful week, Emily found herself clashing with her ten-year-old son, Noah, over homework. Noah often resisted doing his assignments, preferring to play video games instead. One evening, after a long day at work, Emily lost her patience and raised her voice, telling Noah that he was going to fail if he didn't take his homework seriously. Noah responded with anger, slamming his book shut and shouting, "I hate homework!" Both mother and son felt hurt and frustrated by the exchange.

Later that night, after reflecting on the situation, Emily realized that her approach had only escalated the conflict. She decided to try a more mindful approach the next day. When Noah came home from school, Emily sat down with him and said, "I'm sorry about last night. I know I was really stressed, and I didn't handle things well. Let's talk about how we can make homework time better for both of us." Together, they discussed what was making homework difficult for Noah and came up with a plan that included short breaks and a reward system for completed assignments. By acknowledging her own role in the conflict and working with Noah to find a solution, Emily not only resolved the immediate issue but also strengthened their relationship.

Steps for Mindful Conflict Resolution

1. **Acknowledge the Conflict Calmly:**
   - **How to do it:** When a conflict arises, calmly acknowledge that there is a problem. This sets the stage for a constructive conversation rather than an emotional escalation.
   - **Example:** If your child refuses to clean their room, instead of immediately issuing a punishment, you might say, "I see that you're upset about cleaning your room. Let's talk about why it's important and how we can make it easier."
2. **Own Your Part:**

- How to do it: Reflect on your own behavior and emotions during the conflict. If you contributed to the escalation, acknowledge your role and apologize if necessary. This models accountability and shows that everyone makes mistakes.
- **Example:** After arguing with your child about screen time, you might say, "I realize that I was really short with you earlier, and I'm sorry for that. I should have listened to your point of view before making a decision."

3. **Focus on Solutions, Not Blame:**
   - **How to do it:** Shift the focus from who's at fault to how the conflict can be resolved. Work together to find a solution that meets both your needs and your child's.
   - **Example:** If your child is upset about a family rule, instead of saying, "That's just the rule, and you have to follow it," you might say, "I understand why this rule feels unfair to you. Let's talk about why it's important and see if there's a way to make it work for both of us."

4. **Stay Present and Listen:**
   - **How to do it:** During the conflict resolution process, stay present and listen to your child's perspective. Avoid interrupting or dismissing their feelings, even if you don't agree with them.
   - **Example:** If your teenager is angry about a curfew, listen to their reasons without immediately shutting them down. After they've expressed their concerns, you can calmly explain your perspective and work together to find common ground.

5. **Follow Up and Reflect:**

- o **How to do it:** After the conflict has been resolved, take time to reflect on what worked and what didn't. Follow up with your child to ensure that the solution is working and to reinforce positive communication habits.
- o **Example:** A few days after resolving a conflict about chores, you might check in with your child and say, "How are you feeling about the new plan we made for chores? Is there anything that's not working for you?" This follow-up shows that you're committed to ongoing communication and improvement.

Mindful communication is the cornerstone of a strong, healthy relationship with your child. By practicing active listening, speaking with empathy, and resolving conflicts mindfully, you create an environment where your child feels valued, understood, and supported. As you continue to develop these communication skills, you'll find that they not only enhance your relationship with your child but also bring greater peace and harmony to your entire family. Remember, the goal of mindful communication is not to be perfect, but to be present—to show up with an open heart, ready to listen, understand, and connect. Each conversation is an opportunity to deepen your bond and to teach your child the invaluable skills of empathy, respect, and emotional intelligence.

Chapter 4: Creating a Mindful Home Environment

The Physical Space

A home is more than just a physical space; it's the emotional and psychological center of your family's life. It's where your child learns, grows, and experiences the world for the first time. A mindful home environment is one that fosters peace, connection, and intentionality. It's a space where every member of the family feels safe, respected, and valued. In this chapter, we'll explore how to create a home that not only supports your child's development but also nurtures your family's well-being through mindfulness.

Your home's physical environment plays a significant role in shaping the experiences and interactions that occur within it. A mindful home is not necessarily about having a perfectly tidy or aesthetically pleasing space—it's about creating an environment that feels welcoming, nurturing, and reflective of your family's values.

Scenario: Transforming Chaos into Calm

Imagine the scene: it's late afternoon, and the living room is a whirlwind of toys, books, and unfolded laundry. The TV is on, and the noise level is climbing as your children play and argue in equal measure. You feel the tension in your shoulders rising as you try to restore order amidst the chaos. In moments like this, it's easy to feel overwhelmed by the physical clutter, which often mirrors the mental clutter in your mind.

Now, picture a different scenario. Instead of trying to tidy everything at once, you take a moment to breathe and observe the space around you. You notice that the clutter is contributing to your stress, and you decide to make a few small, intentional changes. You turn off the TV and encourage your children to help you create designated play areas. You set up a cozy reading nook with cushions and a basket of favorite books. You organize the toys into bins, making it easier for everyone to clean up after playing. As the living room transforms, you feel a sense of calm returning. The space now feels more inviting and less chaotic, making it easier for your family to relax and connect.

Steps to Creating a Mindful Physical Space

1. **Declutter with Intention:**
   - **How to do it:** Start by decluttering areas of your home that tend to accumulate "stuff." This doesn't mean getting rid of everything, but rather keeping only what adds value or brings joy to your family. Involve your children in this process by encouraging them to let go of toys or clothes they no longer use, making space for what truly matters.
   - **Example:** On a Saturday morning, you and your children decide to tackle the playroom. Together, you sort through toys, books, and games, setting aside items to donate or recycle. By the end of the day, the playroom is organized and more spacious, making it easier for the kids to find and enjoy their favorite activities.

2. **Create Calm Zones:**
   - **How to do it:** Designate areas in your home for relaxation and mindfulness. This could be a corner with cushions for meditation, a quiet space with soft lighting for reading, or even a spot by a window where your family can sit and enjoy the view. These calm zones become retreats where both you and your children can take a break from the busyness of daily life.
   - **Example:** After noticing that your daughter, Sophie, often feels overwhelmed after school, you create a "calm corner" in her room. You add a beanbag chair, a soft blanket, and a few of her favorite books. Whenever Sophie feels stressed, she retreats to this corner to decompress, helping her transition smoothly from school to home life.

3. **Incorporate Elements of Nature:**
   - **How to do it:** Bringing elements of nature into your home can enhance the sense of calm and connection. Houseplants, natural light, and outdoor views all contribute to a serene environment. Nature has a grounding effect that can help you and your children feel more centered and at peace.
   - **Example:** You place a few potted plants in the living room and set up a bird feeder outside the window. The greenery and the birds attracted to the feeder create a soothing atmosphere that the whole family enjoys. You find that everyone spends more time in that room, simply appreciating the natural elements.

4. **Mindful Decor:**

- o **How to do it:** Choose decor that reflects your family's values and brings a sense of peace to your home. This might include family photos, artwork that resonates with you, or meaningful objects that inspire reflection. These touches make your home not just a place to live, but a space that nurtures your family's well-being.
- o **Example:** After a family vacation that brought everyone closer, you decide to create a gallery wall in the hallway with photos from the trip. Each time you walk by, you're reminded of the joyful memories you made together, reinforcing a sense of connection and shared experiences.

Daily Routines and Rituals: The Heartbeat of Family Life

Routines and rituals provide structure, comfort, and a sense of belonging within a family. When infused with mindfulness, these daily practices become moments of connection and presence, transforming the ordinary into something meaningful.

Scenario: Morning Mindfulness

The morning rush is a familiar challenge for many families. Getting everyone out the door on time, with lunches packed and shoes tied, can feel like a daily battle. But what if, instead of rushing through the morning, you created a mindful routine that set a positive tone for the day ahead?

Let's imagine a typical morning in your home. Instead of hurriedly waking your children, you start the day with a few minutes of quiet reflection for yourself. You then wake your children gently, taking a moment to sit with them as they transition from sleep to wakefulness. Breakfast becomes a time to connect, with everyone sharing something they're looking forward to that day. Before leaving the house, you take a few deep breaths together, grounding yourselves for the day ahead. This mindful morning routine not only reduces stress but also strengthens your family's bond, making the start of each day a little brighter.

Establishing Mindful Routines

1. **Morning Rituals:**
   - **How to do it:** Start the day with intention by incorporating mindfulness into your morning routine. This could be a few minutes of quiet reflection, a family breakfast where everyone shares something they're grateful for, or a simple breathing exercise before heading out the door. These practices set a positive tone for the day ahead.
   - **Example:** The Thompson family begins each day with a "gratitude breakfast." As they eat, each person shares one thing they're thankful for. This simple practice not only brings the family closer but also helps them start the day with a positive mindset.
2. **Mindful Meals:**
   - **How to do it:** Mealtimes offer a perfect opportunity for mindfulness. Encourage your family to be fully present during meals by turning off the TV, putting away devices, and focusing on the food

and conversation. Take a moment before eating to express gratitude for the meal and the company.

- o **Example:** The Harris family decides to make dinner a screen-free time. They sit together, take a deep breath before starting, and each shares something about their day. This mindful approach to meals helps them connect more deeply and enjoy their time together.

3. **Evening Wind-Down:**
   - o **How to do it:** Create an evening routine that helps your family transition from the busyness of the day to a state of relaxation. This might include a family walk, reading time, or a short meditation. These rituals signal to your body and mind that it's time to unwind, making bedtime smoother for everyone.
   - o **Example:** Every evening after dinner, the Parker family takes a 15-minute walk around the neighborhood. This time together allows them to decompress from the day and enjoy each other's company. By the time they return home, everyone feels calmer and more prepared for bed.

4. **Bedtime Rituals:**
   - o **How to do it:** End the day with a mindful bedtime routine that promotes relaxation and connection. This could involve reading a book together, discussing the highlights of the day, or practicing deep breathing exercises before sleep. These rituals help your child feel secure and loved, setting the stage for a restful night.
   - o **Example:** Lydia and her son, Max, have a special bedtime routine. After reading a book together,

they spend a few minutes talking about the best part of their day. They then take three deep breaths together, which helps Max feel calm and ready for sleep.

Family Connection Rituals: Strengthening Bonds Through Shared Experiences

In addition to daily routines, family rituals—regular activities or traditions that you do together—can strengthen your bond and create lasting memories. These rituals don't have to be elaborate; what matters most is the sense of togetherness they foster.

Scenario: The Power of Tradition

Every Sunday evening, the Millers gather for their weekly family meeting. It's a simple ritual, but one that everyone looks forward to. They start by discussing the week ahead, planning meals, activities, and responsibilities. Each person has a chance to speak, and everyone's voice is heard. After the practical matters are settled, they spend time reflecting on the week that just passed—sharing successes, discussing challenges, and expressing gratitude. The meeting ends with a family activity, like playing a board game or watching a movie together. This weekly ritual not only keeps the family organized but also deepens their connection and helps them navigate the ups and downs of life together.

Creating Family Rituals

1. **Weekly Family Meetings:**
   - **How to do it:** Set aside time each week for a family meeting. This is a space where everyone can share their thoughts, plan the week ahead, and discuss

any issues in a calm and supportive environment. It's a great way to ensure everyone's voice is heard and to strengthen family communication.

- **Example:** The Garcia family holds a weekly meeting every Sunday evening. They start by going over the schedule for the week, then each person shares one thing they're looking forward to and one challenge they're facing. The meeting concludes with a fun activity, like baking cookies or playing a game.

2. **Seasonal Traditions:**

- **How to do it:** Create traditions that mark the changing seasons and bring your family together in celebration. These could be as simple as a fall hike to enjoy the changing leaves, a winter evening spent decorating the house, or a springtime gardening day.

- **Example:** Every autumn, the Roberts family spends a day at the local orchard, picking apples and making homemade cider. This tradition marks the start of fall for them and provides a special time for the family to connect and enjoy the season's bounty.

3. **Mindful Celebrations:**

- **How to do it:** Incorporate mindfulness into your family's celebrations. Whether it's a birthday, holiday, or other special occasion, take time to reflect on the meaning of the event and express gratitude for the people you're celebrating with.

- **Example:** On each family member's birthday, the Wilsons begin the day with a "birthday gratitude circle." They gather together, and everyone shares something they appreciate about the birthday person. This practice adds a meaningful touch to their celebrations and strengthens their bonds.

4. **Monthly Family Outings:**
   - **How to do it:** Plan a monthly outing that everyone in the family can enjoy. This could be a trip to a museum, a hike, a visit to the zoo, or simply a picnic in the park. These outings create shared experiences and memories that bring your family closer.
   - **Example:** The Johnson family has a tradition of "Adventure Sundays," where they explore a new place or try a new activity each month. Whether it's visiting a nearby town or going on a nature walk, these outings give them the chance to discover new things together and enjoy quality time as a family.

Fostering Emotional Safety and Open Communication

A mindful home is one where every family member feels emotionally safe—where they can express their feelings, share their thoughts, and be themselves without fear of judgment or criticism. Creating this kind of environment requires intentional communication and a commitment to listening with empathy.

Scenario: Building Trust Through Open Communication

Sarah and her husband, James, have two children: an eight-year-old daughter named Mia and a twelve-year-old son named Ethan. Over the years, they've worked hard to create an open and trusting relationship with their kids. They've established a family rule that no topic is off-limits—anything can be discussed openly and honestly. When Mia came home from school one day, upset about a disagreement with a friend, she didn't hesitate to talk to her parents about it. She knew that they would listen without judgment, offer support, and help her navigate her feelings. This openness made Mia feel secure in her relationship with her parents, knowing that she could come to them with any problem, big or small.

Building Emotional Safety in Your Home

1. **Encourage Open Dialogue:**
   - **How to do it:** Let your children know that they can talk to you about anything—no matter how difficult or uncomfortable the topic might be. Create a judgment-free zone where they feel safe expressing their thoughts and feelings.
   - **Example:** At dinner one night, ten-year-old Sam asks his parents about a topic he heard at school that made him uncomfortable. His parents listen calmly, ask him how he feels about it, and offer information and reassurance. By handling the situation with openness and care, they reinforce that Sam can come to them with any concern.
2. **Validate Feelings:**
   - **How to do it:** When your child expresses an emotion, validate it, even if you don't fully understand or agree with their perspective. This

shows them that their feelings are important and worthy of attention.

- o **Example:** When Emma's daughter, Lily, came home upset because she wasn't chosen for the school play, Emma said, "I can see how disappointed you are. It's okay to feel sad about this." This validation helped Lily feel understood and less alone in her disappointment.

3. **Practice Non-Judgmental Listening:**
   - o **How to do it:** When your child talks to you, listen without jumping to conclusions or offering immediate advice. Give them the space to express themselves fully before responding.
   - o **Example:** After a tough day at school, fourteen-year-old Alex tells his dad, "I really messed up my math test today." Instead of immediately offering advice or expressing disappointment, Alex's dad says, "That sounds frustrating. Do you want to talk about what happened?" This non-judgmental approach encourages Alex to open up and discuss the issue further.

4. **Model Emotional Honesty:**
   - o **How to do it:** Be open with your own emotions, modeling how to express feelings in a healthy and constructive way. This teaches your child that it's okay to have emotions and that they can be expressed without fear of rejection or ridicule.
   - o **Example:** After a stressful day at work, Maria tells her children, "I'm feeling really tired and a little stressed right now. I'm going to take a few minutes to relax, and then we can talk." By being honest

about her feelings, Maria models emotional transparency and self-care.

Creating a mindful home environment is about more than just organizing your space or establishing routines; it's about fostering a sense of connection, safety, and well-being for every member of your family. By being intentional about the physical space, daily routines, family rituals, and emotional safety, you create a home where mindfulness thrives—where your child feels valued, understood, and supported in their growth. As you continue on your journey of mindful parenting, remember that the environment you create at home is a powerful tool for nurturing your family's well-being. Each moment spent creating a mindful space is an investment in your child's happiness and in the strength of your family's bond.

Chapter 5: Mindful Discipline and Setting Boundaries

Discipline is one of the most challenging aspects of parenting, often fraught with frustration, guilt, and confusion. As parents, we want to guide our children toward positive behavior and help them develop self-control, but finding the right balance between being firm and being compassionate can be difficult. Mindful discipline offers an approach that combines clear boundaries with empathy and understanding. It's about teaching your child responsibility and respect while maintaining a deep connection built on trust and love.

Understanding the Purpose of Discipline

Discipline is not about punishment or exerting control over your child. Rather, it's about teaching and guiding them. The word "discipline" comes from the Latin word "disciplina," which means "instruction" or "knowledge." When approached mindfully, discipline becomes an opportunity to help your child learn important life skills, such as self-regulation, empathy, and problem-solving.

Scenario: Shifting from Punishment to Guidance

Let's consider the story of Jenna, a mother of two boys, Ethan and Lucas. Jenna grew up in a household where discipline was strict and often harsh—mistakes were met with immediate punishment, and little explanation was given. As a result, Jenna was determined to approach discipline differently with her own children. However, she found herself struggling to find an effective way to address misbehavior without resorting to the punitive methods she had experienced.

One day, after a particularly challenging morning in which Ethan refused to get dressed for school, leading to a meltdown, Jenna decided to try something new. Instead of sending Ethan to his room as a punishment, she took a deep breath and sat down with him. She calmly explained why getting dressed on time was important and asked him what was making it difficult for him that morning. Through their conversation, Jenna learned that Ethan was feeling anxious about a test at school. They talked about his worries and came up with a plan to address both his anxiety and the morning routine. By approaching the situation with mindfulness and empathy, Jenna was able to address the underlying issue and guide Ethan toward more positive behavior, all while strengthening their relationship.

Principles of Mindful Discipline

1. **Connection Before Correction:**
   - **How to do it:** Before addressing a misbehavior, take a moment to connect with your child. This connection helps them feel seen and understood, making them more receptive to guidance. By showing empathy first, you open the door to more effective and compassionate discipline.
   - **Example:** When seven-year-old Lily pushes her younger brother out of frustration, instead of immediately scolding her, her father, Tom, takes a deep breath and kneels down to her level. He

gently says, "I can see you're really upset right now. Let's talk about what happened." By connecting with Lily's emotions first, Tom helps her calm down and opens the conversation for a more thoughtful discussion about why pushing isn't acceptable and what she can do instead when she feels frustrated.

2. **Focus on Teaching, Not Punishment:**
   - **How to do it:** Shift the focus of discipline from punishment to teaching. Use each situation as an opportunity to help your child understand the consequences of their actions and to learn better ways to handle similar situations in the future. This approach fosters growth rather than fear or resentment.
   - **Example:** When twelve-year-old Max comes home late without calling, his mother, Rachel, resists the urge to ground him immediately. Instead, she sits down with him and says, "I was really worried when you didn't come home on time, and it's important that we trust each other. Let's talk about what happened and how we can make sure this doesn't happen again." Together, they discuss why communication is important and agree on a plan for the future. Max learns about responsibility and the importance of keeping his word, rather than feeling punished and resentful.

3. **Be Consistent and Clear:**
   - **How to do it:** Children need clear and consistent boundaries to feel secure. When setting rules or expectations, be clear about what is expected and what the consequences will be if those

expectations are not met. Consistency helps your child understand the boundaries and trust that you mean what you say.

- **Example:** The Wilson family has a rule that screen time is allowed only after homework is completed. When their daughter, Mia, tries to negotiate more screen time before finishing her homework, her parents calmly remind her of the rule and the consequence of losing screen time the next day if the rule isn't followed. By staying consistent, Mia learns the importance of completing her responsibilities before enjoying leisure activities.

4. **Use Natural and Logical Consequences:**
   - **How to do it:** Natural consequences are the direct result of a child's behavior, while logical consequences are related and relevant to the misbehavior. These consequences teach your child that their actions have real effects and help them understand the importance of making better choices.
   - **Example:** When Sophie refuses to wear her coat on a chilly day, her mother allows her to experience the natural consequence of feeling cold. She brings the coat along, and when Sophie eventually asks for it, her mother calmly explains why wearing it in the first place would have been a better choice. This experience helps Sophie understand the importance of dressing appropriately for the weather, without feeling shamed or punished.

5. **Encourage Problem-Solving:**
   - **How to do it:** Involve your child in finding solutions to the problems their behavior creates. This not

only teaches responsibility but also empowers them to make better decisions in the future. Encouraging problem-solving helps your child feel capable and respected.

- o **Example:** When Sam repeatedly leaves his toys scattered around the house, his mother, Laura, sits down with him and says, "I've noticed that your toys are all over the place, and it's making it hard to keep the house tidy. What do you think we can do to make sure your toys are put away at the end of the day?" Together, they come up with a plan where Sam sets a timer every evening as a reminder to clean up. By involving Sam in the solution, Laura helps him take ownership of his actions and learn the importance of maintaining a tidy space.

Handling Tantrums and Challenging Behaviors

Tantrums and challenging behaviors are inevitable parts of childhood. While these moments can be frustrating and exhausting, they are also opportunities to teach your child important life skills, such as emotional regulation and problem-solving. Mindful discipline involves approaching these situations with calmness and empathy, helping your child navigate their emotions while reinforcing positive behavior.

Scenario: Navigating a Public Meltdown

Picture this: You're in the grocery store with your three-year-old son, Jack. Everything is going smoothly until you pass the candy aisle. Jack spots his favorite candy and immediately asks for it. When you say no, his face crumples, and within seconds, he's on the floor, kicking and screaming. You can feel the eyes of other shoppers on you, and the stress of the situation begins to mount.

In this moment, it's tempting to react out of frustration or embarrassment. But instead, you take a deep breath and remind yourself that this is an opportunity to practice mindful discipline. You kneel down next to Jack and calmly say, "I see that you're really upset because you can't have the candy right now. It's hard when we don't get what we want, isn't it?" You stay with him, maintaining a calm and compassionate demeanor, and after a few moments, Jack begins to calm down. Once he's calm, you explain again why he can't have the candy and offer him a choice: "We can either finish our shopping quietly, or we can leave the store and try again later. What do you think?" By handling the situation with mindfulness, you help Jack learn to manage his emotions and make better choices, all while maintaining your connection with him.

Strategies for Handling Tantrums Mindfully

1. **Stay Calm and Present:**
   - **How to do it:** When your child is having a tantrum, it's crucial to remain calm and present. Reacting with anger or frustration can escalate the situation, while staying calm helps to de-escalate it. Remember that tantrums are a normal part of development and often occur because children lack the skills to express their emotions in other ways.
   - **Example:** When her toddler, Mia, throws a tantrum in the middle of the living room, Maria feels her own frustration rising. Instead of reacting, she takes a deep breath, kneels down to Mia's level,

and says in a soothing tone, "I see you're really upset right now. Let's take a moment together." Maria's calm demeanor helps Mia begin to calm down as well, allowing them to address the issue more constructively.

2. **Validate Their Feelings:**
   o **How to do it:** Even in the midst of a tantrum, it's important to acknowledge your child's emotions. This doesn't mean giving in to their demands, but it does mean letting them know that you understand how they're feeling. Validation helps your child feel seen and understood, which can make it easier for them to calm down.
   o **Example:** When four-year-old Lily starts crying because she can't have a second cookie, her father, Tom, validates her feelings by saying, "I know you really want another cookie, and it's hard to wait until later." He doesn't give her the cookie, but his acknowledgment helps Lily feel understood, which eventually helps her calm down.

3. **Set Boundaries with Compassion:**
   o **How to do it:** While it's important to validate feelings, it's also essential to set and maintain boundaries. Do this with kindness and firmness, ensuring that your child knows you are there to support them even when they don't get what they want. Setting boundaries teaches your child that their feelings are valid, but that not all behavior is acceptable.
   o **Example:** When Ethan hits his younger brother out of frustration, his mother, Sarah, steps in and says, "I see that you're really upset, but hitting is not

okay. Let's talk about what's bothering you, and we can find a better way to handle it." By setting a clear boundary while also acknowledging Ethan's feelings, Sarah teaches him that while his emotions are understandable, there are appropriate ways to express them.

4. **Offer Choices:**
   - **How to do it:** Giving your child choices within the limits you've set can help them feel a sense of control, which can reduce the intensity of tantrums. These choices should be simple and related to the situation, allowing your child to have some agency while still adhering to the boundaries you've established.
   - **Example:** When five-year-old Emma refuses to put on her shoes, her mother, Laura, gives her two choices: "You can put on your shoes now, or you can carry them and put them on when we get to the car. Which would you like to do?" By offering Emma a choice, Laura helps her feel more in control, which reduces resistance and encourages cooperation.

5. **Reflect and Repair:**
   - **How to do it:** After the tantrum has passed and your child is calm, take time to reflect on what happened and discuss it with them. This is an opportunity to repair any hurt feelings, reinforce the lesson, and help your child understand how they can handle similar situations better in the future.
   - **Example:** Later that evening, after Max has calmed down from a tantrum over screen time, his father,

Jake, sits down with him and says, "I know you were really upset earlier when I said it was time to turn off the TV. Let's talk about what happened and how we can handle it differently next time." Together, they discuss Max's feelings and come up with a plan for managing screen time that works for both of them.

Cultivating Self-Discipline in Your Child

One of the ultimate goals of discipline is to help your child develop self-discipline—the ability to regulate their own behavior, make good decisions, and take responsibility for their actions. Mindful discipline fosters self-discipline by encouraging children to think critically about their choices and learn from their experiences.

Scenario: Encouraging Responsibility

Twelve-year-old Ava is a bright, creative girl, but she often struggles with keeping her room tidy and staying on top of her homework. Her parents, Mark and Lisa, have tried various strategies to help her, from setting up chore charts to offering rewards, but nothing seems to stick. Instead of continuing to remind her or stepping in to clean up for her, Mark and Lisa decide to try a new approach.

They sit down with Ava and explain that they trust her to manage her responsibilities, but that with that trust comes the need to take ownership of her actions. They work together to create a daily routine that includes time for homework and tidying up, and they set up a weekly check-in to see how things are going. Over time, Ava begins to take more initiative in keeping her room clean and completing her assignments, motivated by the sense of responsibility and trust her parents have placed in her. This approach helps Ava develop self-discipline, which will serve her well as she navigates the challenges of adolescence and beyond.

Strategies for Encouraging Self-Discipline

1. **Set Clear Expectations:**
   - **How to do it:** Clearly communicate what you expect from your child in terms of behavior and responsibilities. Make sure they understand the reasons behind these expectations and how they contribute to the well-being of the family.
   - **Example:** Before starting a new school year, the Carter family sits down to discuss expectations for homework, chores, and screen time. By involving their children in the conversation and explaining the reasons behind the rules, they ensure that everyone is on the same page.
2. **Encourage Independence:**
   - **How to do it:** Give your child opportunities to make decisions and take responsibility for their actions. Encourage them to solve problems on their own before stepping in to help. This fosters a sense of independence and confidence in their abilities.
   - **Example:** When nine-year-old Jack forgets his lunch at home, instead of rushing to bring it to him, his parents let him experience the natural consequence of his forgetfulness. Later, they discuss how he can remember his lunch in the future, such as by creating a checklist before

leaving the house. This experience teaches Jack to take responsibility for his belongings.

3. **Reinforce Positive Behavior:**
   - **How to do it:** Acknowledge and reinforce positive behavior when you see it. This doesn't mean constantly praising your child, but rather recognizing their efforts and progress in a meaningful way. Positive reinforcement encourages them to continue making good choices.
   - **Example:** When Ava consistently completes her homework on time for a week, her parents acknowledge her effort by saying, "We're really proud of how responsible you've been with your homework this week. Keep up the great work!" This positive reinforcement motivates Ava to maintain her new habit.

4. **Model Self-Discipline:**
   - **How to do it:** Children learn by watching their parents. Model self-discipline in your own behavior by setting goals, following through on commitments, and managing your own emotions. This shows your child that self-discipline is a valuable skill worth developing.
   - **Example:** When Mark commits to exercising regularly, he sets a schedule and sticks to it, even when he doesn't feel like it. His children see his dedication and learn that self-discipline involves making choices that align with long-term goals, even when it's challenging.

5. **Encourage Reflection:**
   - **How to do it:** Help your child reflect on their behavior and the consequences of their actions.

Encourage them to think about what they could do differently next time and how they can make better choices in the future.

- o **Example:** After a difficult week where Ethan struggled with managing his time, his mother, Jenna, sits down with him to reflect on what went wrong and what he could do differently next week. They discuss setting priorities, making a schedule, and finding ways to stay focused. This reflection helps Ethan learn from his mistakes and develop better self-discipline.

Mindful discipline is about guiding your child with empathy, respect, and consistency. It's about setting boundaries that teach responsibility and self-discipline, while also maintaining a deep connection built on trust and understanding. By approaching discipline mindfully, you help your child learn from their experiences, develop important life skills, and grow into a responsible, self-regulated individual. Remember that discipline is not just about correcting behavior, but about teaching your child how to navigate the world with confidence, compassion, and integrity. Each moment of discipline is an opportunity to reinforce your child's sense of security, self-worth, and belonging within the family.

Chapter 6: Developing Impulse Control

Understanding Impulses in Parenting

Impulse control is a skill that many parents wish they had more of. It's those moments when you find yourself snapping at your child after a long day, or when you give in to demands just to avoid a tantrum, that make you realize how challenging it can be to manage your reactions. But these moments are also opportunities—opportunities to pause, breathe, and choose a response that aligns with your values rather than reacting out of frustration or fatigue.

Let's take a moment to imagine a typical scenario. It's 5:30 PM, and you're in the middle of preparing dinner. Your three-year-old, Katie, is tugging at your leg, asking for a snack even though dinner is just minutes away. You've had a long day at work, the sink is full of dirty dishes, and you can feel the tension building in your shoulders. In a split second, you snap, "Katie, not now! Can't you see I'm busy?" The words come out sharper than you intended, and immediately, you see the hurt in her eyes. She retreats, and you're left with a sinking feeling of regret.

Now, let's rewind that scenario. Imagine the same situation, but instead of reacting on impulse, you take a deep breath. You notice the tension in your body, the irritation bubbling up inside you. You gently place the knife down, turn to Katie, kneel so you're at eye level, and say softly, "I know you're hungry, sweetheart. Dinner will be ready soon. How about you help me set the table while we wait?" Katie, now feeling seen and valued, eagerly agrees. The moment of connection, instead of disconnection, changes the entire evening's tone.

Impulse control in parenting isn't about suppressing your emotions—it's about recognizing them, giving yourself the space to pause, and choosing how to respond in a way that aligns with the kind of parent you want to be. It's about transforming those moments of potential conflict into opportunities for connection.

Strategies for Developing Impulse Control

1. The Power of the Pause

The pause is your best friend when it comes to managing impulses. It's that brief moment between the trigger and your reaction—a moment that can change everything. But pausing isn't easy, especially when you're stressed or tired. It requires practice, and it starts with being aware of your triggers.

Example: Imagine a father, Tom, who struggles with his temper, especially during the evening when his patience is wearing thin. His six-year-old son, Ben, often resists bedtime, leading to a nightly battle of wills. One evening, Tom feels his anger rising as Ben stalls once again, asking for another story. In the past, Tom might have snapped, raising his voice and demanding compliance. But this time, Tom notices the familiar signs of frustration—his clenched jaw, the quickening of his breath. Instead of reacting, he pauses. He takes a deep breath, closes his eyes for a moment, and then kneels beside Ben. "I can see you're not ready for bed yet," Tom says gently. "But it's time to rest so we can have more fun tomorrow. How about we sing a lullaby together instead of reading another story?" Ben, sensing his father's calmness, agrees. The evening ends on a peaceful note, and Tom feels a deep sense of satisfaction for having handled the situation differently.

2. Breathing Techniques

Breathing is a simple yet powerful tool for managing impulses. When you feel anger or frustration rising, a few deep breaths can help calm your nervous system and give you the space to choose a more mindful response.

Scenario: Jessica is a mother of two young boys, ages four and seven. After a long day at work, she picks up her children from daycare, only to find them bickering in the backseat of the car. The noise grates on her already frazzled nerves. Her first instinct is to shout at them to be quiet, but instead, she takes a deep breath, focusing on the feeling of the air filling her lungs and slowly releasing the tension with her exhale. She repeats this a few times, and as she does, she feels her frustration begin to subside. Now calmer, Jessica turns to her boys and says, "I can see you're both upset. Let's take turns telling me what's going on, and we'll figure it out together." Her calmness helps to defuse the situation, and soon, the car is filled with conversation instead of conflict.

3. Mindful Observation of Triggers

Understanding what triggers your impulses is key to managing them. Triggers can be anything from certain behaviors, like whining or defiance, to situations where you feel overwhelmed or out of control. By identifying your triggers, you can anticipate challenging moments and prepare yourself to respond mindfully.

Example: Rachel, a stay-at-home mom, often finds herself feeling overwhelmed by the constant demands of her three young children. She notices that she's particularly irritable in the late afternoon, when everyone seems to need something from her at once. Recognizing this pattern, Rachel starts to implement a mindful observation practice. Each afternoon, she sets a timer for five minutes and sits quietly, simply noticing her thoughts and feelings without judgment. She begins to realize that her irritability often stems from feeling inadequate and not having enough time for herself. Armed with this insight, Rachel makes a small change to her routine—she starts taking a 10-minute break before the kids get home from school, using that time to rest or enjoy a cup of tea. This small act of self-care helps Rachel feel more grounded and less reactive during the busy hours that follow.

4. Empathy as a Tool for Impulse Control

Sometimes, the most powerful way to manage your impulses is to put yourself in your child's shoes. By imagining what they might be feeling, you can soften your own response and approach the situation with compassion.

Scenario: David, a father of a teenager named Mia, often finds himself frustrated by her reluctance to talk about her day. One evening, after asking about her school day and receiving only a sullen shrug in response, David feels his irritation rising. His first impulse is to demand that she talk to him, but instead, he takes a step back and considers how he might have felt at her age—navigating the emotional minefield of adolescence, feeling misunderstood and pressured. With this perspective, David's approach changes. He gently says, "I remember feeling that way when I was your age. It's okay if you don't want to talk right now.

Just know I'm here when you're ready." This simple acknowledgment of her feelings opens a door, and later that evening, Mia comes to him on her own to share a bit about what's been bothering her.

5. **Journaling for Reflection**

Journaling is a powerful way to reflect on your impulses and identify patterns in your behavior. By writing down your thoughts and feelings, you can gain clarity on what triggers your reactions and explore how you might respond differently in the future.

Example: Maria, a single mother of a nine-year-old son, finds herself frequently losing her temper during homework time. Each evening, the struggle to get her son to focus on his assignments leads to a battle of wills, leaving both of them feeling defeated. Wanting to break this cycle, Maria starts keeping a journal. After each homework session, she writes about what happened, how she felt, and what she might do differently next time. Over time, Maria notices a pattern—her son struggles most on days when he's had a tough time at school. Armed with this insight, Maria changes her approach. Instead of diving straight into homework, she first takes time to talk with her son about his day, offering support and encouragement before tackling the assignments. This shift reduces their evening conflicts and strengthens their relationship.

Teaching Impulse Control to Children

Just as it's important for parents to manage their own impulses, it's equally crucial to teach children how to manage theirs. Impulse control is a skill that develops over time, and parents play a key role in guiding their children through this process.

1. Modeling Behavior

Children learn by watching the adults in their lives. When you model good impulse control, your children are more likely to develop these skills themselves.

Scenario: During a family game night, the Johnson family is playing a board game. When eight-year-old Ethan loses a turn, he starts to get upset, ready to throw the dice across the room. Instead of reprimanding him immediately, his father, Mark, models calmness. He takes a deep breath, looks Ethan in the eye, and says, "I know it's frustrating to lose a turn. Let's take a deep breath together and keep going. We're here to have fun, and the game isn't just about winning." Mark then leads Ethan in a deep breathing exercise, and after a few moments, Ethan is ready to continue the game, having learned a valuable lesson in managing his frustration.

2. Using Stories and Examples

Children often respond well to stories that illustrate the concepts you're trying to teach. Using age-appropriate stories about characters who learn to manage their impulses can help your child understand the importance of this skill.

Example: Sarah reads a bedtime story to her five-year-old daughter, Lucy, about a little bear who learns to wait patiently for his turn at the playground. As they read, Sarah pauses to ask Lucy how the little bear might feel and what he could do to manage his feelings. After the story, they talk about times when Lucy might feel impatient and how she can use her "bear breaths" to help her wait. This story not only entertains but also teaches Lucy a valuable lesson in impulse control.

3. Practicing Self-Regulation Together

Children need opportunities to practice impulse control in a safe and supportive environment. Turn this practice into a game or a fun activity that helps them build these skills without feeling pressured.

Scenario: The Carter family decides to play a game of "Red Light, Green Light" in their backyard. This classic game is not just fun; it's also a great way to practice impulse control. As they play, four-year-old Olivia learns to stop and go on command, developing her ability to control her movements and impulses. Later, when Olivia feels the urge to run in the house, her mother gently reminds her of the game they played and suggests they practice "Red Light, Green Light" walking to the kitchen. This playful approach helps Olivia learn to manage her impulses in a way that feels natural and enjoyable.

4. Encouraging Problem-Solving

Teaching children to think before they act is an important part of developing impulse control. Encourage your child to consider the consequences of their actions and to think of alternative ways to respond to situations.

Example: When seven-year-old Jake feels angry because his sister took his toy, his first instinct is to snatch it back. Instead of intervening immediately, his mother, Laura, encourages him to think about how his sister might feel and to come up with a solution. Together, they brainstorm different ways Jake could handle the situation—asking politely for the toy back, offering to trade toys, or finding something else to play with. This process not only helps Jake control his impulses but also teaches him valuable problem-solving skills.

Chapter 7: Mindful Play and Activities

Engaging with Your Child Mindfully

Play is the language of children. It's through play that they explore the world, express their emotions, and connect with those around them. However, in our busy lives, it's easy to treat playtime as just another task to check off the list, rather than an opportunity for deep connection and learning. Mindful play is about slowing down, being fully present, and embracing these moments of joy and discovery with your child.

Imagine a typical weekend afternoon. You're in the living room with your daughter, Chloe, who is excited to build a castle with her blocks. Your mind, however, is still swirling with thoughts of the errands you need to run, the emails you need to send, and the laundry that's piling up. As Chloe hands you a block, you absentmindedly place it on the castle, barely noticing her animated instructions. She notices your distraction and, feeling the disconnect, becomes frustrated, saying, "You're not even paying attention!"

Now, let's reimagine that scenario with a mindful approach. You take a deep breath, setting aside the mental to-do list, and decide to give Chloe your undivided attention. You sit down next to her, at her level, and really engage. You notice the way her eyes light up as she describes her vision for the castle, the way she carefully selects each block, and the pride in her voice when she places the final piece. You're fully present, sharing in her joy and creativity. Chloe senses this, and her frustration melts away, replaced by a sense of connection and accomplishment. The castle you build together isn't just a structure made of blocks—it's a shared experience, a moment of togetherness that strengthens your bond.

Steps for Mindful Engagement in Play:

1. **Be Fully Present:** When you decide to play with your child, commit to being fully there. Turn off your phone, set aside distractions, and focus solely on the activity. This doesn't just mean physically being there—it means being mentally and emotionally present as well.

   Example: Every evening after dinner, Jenna sets aside 20 minutes for uninterrupted playtime with her son, Max. They do whatever Max chooses, whether it's playing with his toy cars, building a fort, or drawing together. During this time, Jenna focuses solely on Max, asking questions, making observations, and engaging in his world. Max knows that this time is just for him, and it becomes one of the highlights of his day.

2. **Observe and Follow Their Lead:** Children often know exactly what they want to play and how they want to play it. By observing and following your child's lead, you enter their world on their terms, which can be deeply validating for them.

   Scenario: Sarah's daughter, Lily, loves to play pretend, often setting up elaborate tea parties with her stuffed animals. Instead of directing the play or suggesting what should happen next, Sarah lets Lily take charge. She watches as Lily carefully arranges the teacups and assigns roles to each stuffed animal, stepping in only when invited. By following Lily's lead, Sarah honors her daughter's creativity and imagination, making the playtime more meaningful and enjoyable for both of them.

3. **Engage All Your Senses:** Mindful play isn't just about what you see or hear—it's about fully immersing yourself in the experience. Notice the textures, sounds, and even the smells around you. Engage all your senses to deepen your connection with the activity.

   Example: During a rainy afternoon, James and his daughter, Ella, decide to bake cookies together. As they mix the dough, James encourages Ella to notice how the ingredients change as they're combined, how the dough feels between her fingers, and how the kitchen begins to fill with the warm, sweet smell of baking cookies. By engaging all their senses, James and Ella turn a simple baking session into a rich, sensory experience that they both savor.

4. **Embrace Imperfection:** Children's play is often messy, unpredictable, and imperfect—just like life. Embrace this imperfection, and let go of any need for the activity to be orderly or productive. The goal isn't to create something perfect, but to enjoy the process.

   Scenario: During an art session, Ben and his son, Jack, are painting together. Jack enthusiastically splashes paint onto the paper, creating a chaotic swirl of colors. At first, Ben is tempted to guide Jack towards a more "organized" approach, but then he decides to let go and join in. He adds his own splashes of color, laughing as the paint mixes in unexpected ways. The result is a vibrant, messy masterpiece that they both love—not because it's perfect, but because it's theirs.

Mindful Activities for Connection

While play is a natural way for children to engage with the world, there are also specific activities that can enhance mindfulness for both you and your child. These activities are designed to slow things down, bring awareness to the present moment, and foster a deeper connection between you.

1. Mindful Nature Walks

Spending time in nature is a powerful way to practice mindfulness. Nature naturally encourages us to slow down, breathe deeply, and notice the world around us. A mindful walk with your child can be a simple yet profound experience.

Example: Every Saturday morning, Amy and her daughter, Sophie, go for a nature walk in the nearby park. Before they start, they take a moment to close their eyes, take a deep breath, and set an intention to notice as much as they can. As they walk, they pause to observe the details—the rough bark of a tree, the sound of leaves rustling in the wind, the smell of fresh earth after a rain. They talk about what they see and hear, sharing their observations with each other. By the time they return home, both Amy and Sophie feel more grounded, calm, and connected.

2. Mindful Storytelling

Storytelling is a wonderful way to connect with your child, and when done mindfully, it can also be a soothing, grounding activity. Mindful storytelling involves telling a story slowly and deliberately, focusing on the rhythm of the words and the emotions they evoke.

Scenario: At bedtime, instead of reading from a book, Liam decides to tell his son, Noah, a story from his own childhood. He speaks slowly, describing the sights, sounds, and feelings he experienced, allowing Noah to visualize the story vividly. As he tells the story, Liam watches Noah's face, noticing how his eyes widen at the exciting parts and how he smiles at the funny moments. This mindful storytelling not only entertains Noah but also strengthens their bond, as Noah feels more connected to his father's past and experiences.

3. Mindful Breathing Exercises

Mindful breathing is a simple yet powerful practice that can help both you and your child calm down and focus. Teaching your child to connect with their breath can give them a valuable tool for managing stress and emotions.

Example: After a particularly rough day at school, Emily's son, Jake, comes home feeling upset and overwhelmed. Sensing his distress, Emily sits down with him on the couch and suggests they do a "balloon breath" exercise together. She guides him to imagine that his belly is a balloon, slowly inflating as he breathes in and deflating as he breathes out. They practice this for a few minutes, with Emily encouraging Jake to notice how his body feels as he breathes. Gradually, Jake's breathing slows, and he begins to relax. By the end of the exercise, he's feeling calmer and ready to talk about what happened at school.

4. Mindful Art Projects

Art is a natural outlet for creativity and emotion, making it a perfect activity for mindfulness. When you approach art mindfully, the focus shifts from the final product to the process itself, allowing both you and your child to express yourselves freely and fully.

Scenario: On a rainy afternoon, Mia and her daughter, Lily, decide to do some painting. Instead of aiming to create a specific picture, they decide to focus on the experience of painting itself. They choose their colors carefully, notice the way the paintbrush feels in their hands, and watch how the colors blend on the paper. Mia encourages Lily to paint whatever she feels, without worrying about making it look "right." As they paint, they talk about how the colors make them feel, creating a shared moment of creativity and expression. By the end of the session, both Mia and Lily feel more relaxed and connected, their minds as colorful as the paintings they've created.

5. Mindful Listening Games

Listening is a key component of mindfulness, and teaching your child to listen mindfully can help them become more aware of their surroundings and more present in their interactions. Mindful listening games can be a fun way to develop this skill.

Example: During a quiet evening, Emma and her son, Lucas, decide to play a game of "sound bingo." They sit quietly in the living room, close their eyes, and take turns identifying the different sounds they hear—the hum of the refrigerator, the distant sound of a car passing by, the ticking of the clock. Each time they hear a new sound, they quietly name it and share it with the other. This game not only sharpens their listening skills but also brings a sense of calm and focus, as they tune into the subtle sounds of their environment. By the end of the game, both Emma and Lucas feel more attuned to their surroundings and to each other.

Chapter 8: Mindfulness for Parents' Self-Care

Parenting is a demanding, all-encompassing role. Amid the daily chaos of raising children, it's easy to forget about your own needs. However, just as you can't pour from an empty cup, you can't give your best to your children if you're running on empty. Self-care isn't a luxury; it's a necessity. In this chapter, we'll explore how mindfulness can be an essential tool in caring for yourself—physically, emotionally, and mentally—so that you can show up as the best version of yourself for your family.

Why Self-Care Is Essential for Parents

Many parents struggle with the idea of self-care, feeling that it's selfish to focus on their own needs when there's so much to do for their children. However, self-care is not about indulging yourself at the expense of your family; it's about ensuring that you have the energy, patience, and emotional resilience to be the parent you want to be.

Scenario: The Impact of Neglecting Self-Care

Let's consider Sarah, a mother of three who juggles a demanding job with her family responsibilities. From the moment she wakes up, she's in motion—preparing meals, getting the kids ready for school, working long hours, and then coming home to more tasks. Sarah rarely has time for herself, and over time, she begins to feel drained and overwhelmed. She notices that she's becoming more irritable with her children and less patient with her partner.

Despite her best efforts, she feels like she's constantly running on empty.

One evening, after a particularly challenging day, Sarah snaps at her daughter for a minor mistake. Immediately, she feels guilty and ashamed of her outburst. That night, as she reflects on the day, Sarah realizes that she's been neglecting her own needs for far too long. She decides to make a change—not just for her own sake, but for her family's as well. She starts by carving out a few minutes each day for herself, practicing deep breathing and mindfulness to center herself. Over time, these small acts of self-care help Sarah feel more balanced and resilient, allowing her to approach parenting with renewed energy and patience.

Practical Self-Care Practices for Parents:

Self-care doesn't have to be time-consuming or complicated. It's about finding small, meaningful ways to care for your body, mind, and spirit. Mindfulness can be a powerful tool in this process, helping you stay grounded and present as you navigate the challenges of parenting.

1. **Morning Rituals for Centering Yourself**

Starting your day with a simple self-care ritual can set a positive tone for the rest of the day. This could be as simple as enjoying a quiet cup of tea before the kids wake up, doing a few stretches to wake up your body, or spending five minutes in meditation.

Example: Every morning, before her children wake up, Lisa spends ten minutes in quiet meditation. She sits in a comfortable chair, closes her eyes, and focuses on her breath. Some days, her mind races with thoughts of the day ahead, but she gently brings her focus back to her breathing. Other days, she feels a deep sense of peace and clarity. This small ritual helps Lisa start her day with calmness and intention, making it easier to navigate the challenges that arise.

2. Mindful Moments Throughout the Day

In the midst of a busy day, it's easy to lose yourself in the demands of parenting and work. But by taking mindful moments throughout the day, you can stay connected to yourself and your needs.

Scenario: During a particularly hectic day, Mark finds himself feeling overwhelmed and irritable. Instead of pushing through the stress, he decides to take a "mindful minute." He steps outside, takes a deep breath, and focuses on the feeling of the sun on his face and the sound of the birds in the trees. For that one minute, he lets go of everything else and just exists in the moment. When he returns to his tasks, he feels calmer and more grounded, ready to tackle the rest of the day with renewed energy.

3. Evening Wind-Down Rituals

Just as it's important to start your day mindfully, it's equally important to end it that way. Creating an evening wind-down ritual can help you let go of the day's stresses and prepare for a restful night.

Example: After putting her children to bed, Rachel spends ten minutes journaling. She writes about her day—the challenges, the joys, the moments of connection with her children. She also writes about what she's grateful for, even on the tough days. This practice helps Rachel process her emotions, clear her mind, and end her day on a positive note. By the time she goes to bed, she feels a sense of peace, ready to rest and recharge.

4. Connecting with Nature

Nature has a way of calming the mind and nourishing the soul. Spending time outside, even if it's just for a few minutes, can be a powerful form of self-care.

Scenario: Emma has always loved the outdoors, but since becoming a mother, she rarely finds the time to enjoy it. One afternoon, feeling particularly stressed, she decides to take her son to the park. While he plays, Emma takes off her shoes and walks barefoot on the grass, feeling the cool earth beneath her feet. She watches the trees sway in the breeze, listens to the birds, and breathes in the fresh air. These few moments of connection with nature rejuvenate her, reminding her of the importance of caring for herself as she cares for her family.

5. Mindful Reading and Reflection

Taking time to read and reflect on your experiences can be a deeply restorative form of self-care. Whether it's a book that inspires you, a poem that moves you, or a simple reflection on your day, this practice can help you reconnect with yourself.

Example: Each night before bed, Tom spends fifteen minutes reading a book that inspires him. Sometimes it's a novel, other times it's a book on mindfulness or parenting. After reading, he takes a few minutes to reflect on what he's read and how it applies to his life. This quiet time helps Tom unwind and gain new insights, making him feel more centered and prepared for the challenges of the next day.

Self-Compassion: The Heart of Self-Care

In addition to physical self-care, emotional self-care is crucial for parents. Parenting is full of ups and downs, and it's easy to be hard on yourself when things don't go as planned. Practicing self-compassion allows you to acknowledge your struggles without judgment and to treat yourself with the same kindness you would offer to a friend.

Scenario: Embracing Self-Compassion

Tom is a father who prides himself on being patient and supportive with his children. However, after a particularly stressful week, he finds himself losing his temper more often than usual. One evening, after raising his voice at his son, Tom feels a wave of guilt and self-criticism wash over him. He starts thinking, "I'm a terrible father. I should have more control over my emotions."

But instead of letting these thoughts spiral, Tom takes a different approach. He remembers something he read about self-compassion and decides to try it. He sits down, places his hand on his heart, and silently says to himself, "This is hard. Parenting is tough, and it's okay to feel this way. I'm doing my best." Tom takes a few deep breaths, allowing the tension to ease, and resolves to approach the next day with a fresh perspective. By practicing self-compassion, Tom is able to move past his guilt and focus on being the parent he aspires to be.

Exercises for Cultivating Self-Compassion:

1. **Self-Compassion Meditation:** Spend a few minutes each day practicing self-compassion meditation. Sit quietly,

place your hand on your heart, and silently repeat phrases like, "May I be kind to myself," "May I accept myself as I am," and "May I find peace and strength." This practice can help you develop a kinder, more compassionate relationship with yourself.

2. **Loving-Kindness Practice:** In a quiet moment, close your eyes and bring to mind someone you care about. Silently send them well-wishes, such as "May you be happy," "May you be healthy," and "May you live with ease." After a few minutes, turn these well-wishes towards yourself, offering the same kindness and compassion to your own heart.

3. **Journaling for Self-Compassion:** At the end of each day, write down three things you appreciate about yourself or something you did well that day. This could be as simple as, "I was patient with my child today," or "I took time to care for myself." Reflecting on these positive moments can help you cultivate a sense of self-worth and compassion.

The Ripple Effect: How Your Self-Care Benefits Your Family

Taking care of yourself is not just beneficial for you—it has a positive impact on your entire family. When you prioritize your well-being, you're better equipped to handle the challenges of parenting with patience, empathy, and resilience. Your children learn from your example, understanding that self-care is a vital part of a healthy, balanced life.

Scenario: Modeling Self-Care for Your Children

Lily is a single mother who has always put her children's needs ahead of her own. Over the years, she's noticed that this approach has taken a toll on her health and happiness. After attending a mindfulness workshop, Lily decides to make self-care a priority. She starts small, taking time each day to meditate, exercise, and enjoy a hobby she loves—painting.

At first, Lily worries that taking time for herself might make her children feel neglected, but the opposite happens. Her children notice that she's happier, more patient, and more engaged when she spends time with them. They start asking about her painting and even join her in creating art. By modeling self-care, Lily teaches her children the importance of taking care of themselves, and the entire family benefits from the positive changes in her well-being.

Creating a Family Culture of Self-Care

1. **Incorporate Self-Care into Family Routines:**
   - **How to do it:** Make self-care a regular part of your family's routine. This could involve family yoga sessions, nature walks, or quiet reading time. By making self-care a shared activity, you reinforce its importance and create positive habits for your children.
   - **Example:** Every Saturday morning, the Hernandez family goes for a hike in the nearby park. This routine not only promotes physical health but also allows the family to connect with nature and each other. The children look forward to these outings, and it becomes a cherished part of their weekly routine.
2. **Encourage Your Children to Practice Self-Care:**
   - **How to do it:** Teach your children about the importance of self-care by encouraging them to

find activities that help them relax and recharge. This could include hobbies, creative activities, or mindfulness practices. Help them understand that taking care of their mental and emotional health is just as important as their physical health.

- **Example:** When her son, Ben, starts feeling stressed about school, Laura encourages him to try deep breathing exercises and journaling as ways to manage his anxiety. She helps him set aside time each day for these practices, and over time, Ben develops a healthy routine that helps him cope with stress more effectively.

3. **Create a Supportive Environment:**
   - **How to do it:** Foster an environment where self-care is encouraged and supported. This means respecting each family member's need for alone time, creating spaces for relaxation, and supporting each other's self-care practices.
   - **Example:** The Lee family designates Sunday afternoons as "quiet time." During this time, each family member chooses a self-care activity, whether it's reading, napping, or practicing a hobby. By respecting each other's need for rest and relaxation, the family creates a culture of self-care that everyone values.

4. **Lead by Example:**
   - **How to do it:** The best way to teach your children about self-care is to practice it yourself. When they see you taking time for yourself, managing stress effectively, and prioritizing your well-being, they learn that self-care is an essential part of life.

- **Example:** After a long day, Mark takes time to unwind by playing his guitar—a hobby he loves but often neglects. His children see him enjoying this time and start to ask about learning to play music themselves. By leading by example, Mark not only benefits his own well-being but also inspires his children to explore their own self-care practices.

Mindful self-care is about recognizing that your well-being is the foundation of your ability to parent effectively. By taking time to care for yourself—physically, emotionally, and mentally—you enhance your capacity to nurture, support, and connect with your children. Self-care is not selfish; it's essential. It allows you to show up as the best version of yourself, ready to meet the challenges of parenting with grace, patience, and love. Remember, when you take care of yourself, you're not just benefiting yourself—you're creating a ripple effect that positively impacts your entire family.

Conclusion: The Journey of Mindful Parenting

Mindful parenting is not about achieving perfection. It's about showing up, every day, with an open heart and a willingness to grow. It's about being present with your child, even when it's hard, and being kind to yourself, even when you stumble. As you practice mindfulness in your parenting, you'll find that it's not just your relationship with your child that deepens—it's your relationship with yourself.

Consider the story of Laura, a mother who, like many, often felt overwhelmed by the demands of parenting. She began practicing mindfulness not as a way to become a perfect parent, but as a way to find more peace and joy in her daily life. Over time, she noticed that she was more patient with her children, more connected with her partner, and more compassionate with herself. The small, mindful moments—pausing to take a breath before responding, listening fully to her children, taking time for self-care—added up to big changes in her family life. Laura's journey is a reminder that mindfulness is not a destination, but a path, one that leads to deeper connection, greater peace, and more joy in the everyday moments of parenting.

As you continue on your own journey of mindful parenting, remember to be gentle with yourself. There will be days when you feel disconnected, frustrated, or overwhelmed, and that's okay. Mindfulness is about accepting each moment as it is, with all its imperfections. Every moment is an opportunity to begin again, to reconnect with your child, and to reconnect with yourself.

Thank you for embarking on this journey of mindful parenting. May you find peace in the present moment, joy in the connection with your child, and compassion for yourself as you navigate the beautiful, messy, and rewarding path of parenthood.

Appendix: Practical Tools and Resources for Mindful Parenting

To help you on your journey of mindful parenting, this appendix offers a variety of practical tools, exercises, and resources that you can incorporate into your daily life. These tools are designed to be simple yet effective, helping you cultivate mindfulness, manage stress, and strengthen your connection with your child.

1. Mindful Breathing Exercises

Balloon Breathing for Kids:

- **How to do it:** Have your child imagine they are blowing up a balloon in their belly. Inhale deeply through the nose, filling up the "balloon" (belly expands), then exhale slowly through the mouth, letting the "air" out (belly contracts). Repeat this 5-10 times.
- **When to use it:** This exercise is great for calming down before bedtime, reducing anxiety before a big event, or simply helping your child relax during a stressful moment.

Three Deep Breaths for Parents:

- **How to do it:** Whenever you feel stressed or overwhelmed, pause and take three deep breaths. Inhale slowly through your nose, hold for a count of three, and exhale slowly through your mouth. Focus solely on your breath, letting go of other thoughts.

- **When to use it:** Use this technique whenever you need a quick reset—before responding to your child in a challenging moment, in the middle of a busy day, or when you need to regain your composure.

2. Mindful Listening Practices

Mindful Listening for Kids:

- **How to do it:** Sit with your child in a quiet space. Ask them to close their eyes and listen carefully to the sounds around them for one minute. Afterward, talk about the sounds they heard—both close by and far away.
- **When to use it:** This exercise is perfect for developing focus and awareness. Try it before a study session, during a nature walk, or as a calming activity before bedtime.

Empathy-Based Listening for Parents:

- **How to do it:** The next time your child is talking to you, practice mindful listening by giving them your full attention. Maintain eye contact, nod or give verbal acknowledgments, and refrain from interrupting. After they've finished, reflect back what you heard to show understanding.
- **When to use it:** Use this practice during important conversations with your child, especially when they are sharing their feelings or discussing something that matters to them.

3. Mindful Communication Exercises

The Calm Jar:

- **How to do it:** Fill a clear jar with water, glitter glue, and a few drops of food coloring. Seal the lid tightly. When your child is upset, shake the jar and encourage them to watch the glitter settle as they take deep breaths.
- **When to use it:** This tool is excellent for helping children calm down after a tantrum or during moments of high emotion. It's a visual and physical way to show how emotions can settle with time and patience.

I-Messages for Parents:

- **How to do it:** Instead of using "You" statements (which can feel accusatory), practice using "I" messages to express your feelings and needs. For example, instead of saying, "You never listen to me," try, "I feel frustrated when I'm not heard."
- **When to use it:** Use I-messages during conflicts or difficult discussions with your child to promote more effective and less confrontational communication.

4. Creating a Mindful Home Environment

Mindful Decluttering Checklist:

- **How to do it:** Tackle one area of your home at a time— whether it's a room, a closet, or just a drawer. Ask yourself (and your children) these questions: Does this item serve a purpose? Does it bring joy? When was the last time it was used? Let go of anything that no longer adds value to your life.
- **When to use it:** Use this checklist during seasonal cleanings, before a move, or anytime you feel your home is becoming cluttered and stressful.

Gratitude Corner:

- **How to do it:** Designate a small area in your home as a Gratitude Corner. Decorate it with meaningful items—photos, artwork, or mementos. Each day, have family members write down something they're grateful for and place it in the corner.
- **When to use it:** Incorporate this practice into your daily routine, perhaps at the end of the day, to foster a sense of appreciation and mindfulness within your family.

5. Mindful Parenting Resources

Books:

- **"The Whole-Brain Child" by Daniel J. Siegel and Tina Payne Bryson:** A practical guide to understanding your child's brain and using that knowledge to foster healthier, more resilient children.
- **"Everyday Blessings: The Inner Work of Mindful Parenting" by Myla and Jon Kabat-Zinn:** A foundational book on the practice of mindful parenting, filled with wisdom and practical advice.

Apps:

- **Headspace for Kids:** Offers a range of guided meditations and mindfulness exercises designed specifically for children.
- **Insight Timer:** A free app with thousands of meditations, including many focused on parenting and mindful living.

Websites and Online Courses:

- **Mindful.org:** A comprehensive resource for mindfulness practices, including sections specifically for parents.
- **The Greater Good Science Center (ggsc.berkeley.edu):** Offers research-based resources and practices for mindfulness, empathy, and emotional intelligence.

Parenting Communities:

- **Mindful Parenting Facebook Groups:** Connect with other parents who are practicing mindfulness in their families. These groups offer support, ideas, and shared experiences.
- **Local Parenting Workshops:** Look for workshops or support groups in your community that focus on mindful parenting, often offered through community centers, schools, or wellness centers.

Final Thoughts: Continuing Your Journey

The journey of mindful parenting is a lifelong one. It's about cultivating presence, empathy, and compassion in your daily interactions with your child and with yourself. It's about recognizing that every moment—whether joyful or challenging—is an opportunity to connect more deeply, to learn, and to grow.

As you continue to practice mindfulness in your parenting, you'll likely encounter obstacles and setbacks. There will be days when mindfulness feels difficult, when stress and fatigue get the better of you, and when your patience wears thin. But these moments are part of the process. They are reminders that mindfulness is not about perfection, but about practice. It's about showing up each day with the intention to be present, to listen deeply, and to respond with kindness.

Remember, too, that you are not alone on this journey. There is a growing community of parents around the world who are also exploring mindful parenting, learning from their experiences, and supporting one another. Reach out, share your experiences, and find inspiration in the stories of others.

Above all, be gentle with yourself. Parenting is one of the most challenging and rewarding endeavors you will ever undertake. By practicing mindfulness, you are not only nurturing your child's growth—you are also nurturing your own. Each mindful breath, each moment of connection, is a step towards creating a more peaceful, loving, and joyful life for you and your family.

Thank you for embarking on this journey. May it bring you and your family closer, and may it help you find greater peace, joy, and connection in the beautiful, messy, and extraordinary adventure of parenting.

Bonus Chapter: Mindful Parenting in Difficult Situations

Parenting is challenging even in the best of times, but there are moments when the difficulties seem overwhelming—whether it's dealing with a child's challenging behavior, managing your own stress, or navigating a family crisis. This bonus chapter offers guidance on how to apply mindful parenting practices in these tough situations, helping you maintain connection, compassion, and presence even when the going gets tough.

1. Navigating Tantrums and Meltdowns

Every parent has faced a moment when their child is in the throes of a full-blown tantrum. It might be in the middle of a grocery store, during a playdate, or right before bedtime. These moments can be incredibly stressful and exhausting, but they are also an opportunity to practice deep mindfulness and compassion.

Scenario: A Supermarket Meltdown

Imagine you're at the supermarket with your four-year-old, James. Everything has been going smoothly until you reach the checkout line. James spots a display of candy bars and asks for one. You calmly explain that it's almost dinner time, and he can't have a candy bar right now. In an instant, his face crumples, and he starts to cry, quickly escalating into a full-blown tantrum. The people around you begin to stare, and you can feel your anxiety rising, your patience wearing thin.

Mindful Response:

1. **Pause and Breathe:** Before reacting, take a deep breath. Feel your feet on the ground, and let the breath anchor you to the present moment. Remind yourself that this is a difficult moment, but you have the tools to handle it.
2. **Acknowledge the Emotion:** Get down to James's level and acknowledge his feelings. "I see you're really upset right now because you can't have the candy bar. It's okay to feel disappointed."
3. **Stay Calm and Present:** Keep your voice calm and steady, even if James's cries continue. You might say, "I'm here with you. Let's take some deep breaths together." Model the deep breathing, encouraging him to follow along.
4. **Offer Comfort and Alternatives:** If James begins to calm down, offer comfort and an alternative. "I know it's hard when you really want something. How about we pick out a piece of fruit for when we get home, or we can make a special dessert together after dinner?"
5. **Be Patient:** If the tantrum continues, stay patient. This is a learning process, both for you and for James. Eventually, his emotions will settle, and you can calmly continue your shopping.

By approaching the situation with mindfulness, you help James learn that his feelings are valid, but there are ways to manage them that don't involve getting what he wants immediately. Over time, these practices build emotional regulation skills in your child, reducing the frequency and intensity of future meltdowns.

2. Managing Parental Stress and Overwhelm

There are times when the demands of parenting, work, and life can feel overwhelming. You might find yourself feeling irritable, exhausted, or even resentful—emotions that can affect your interactions with your child. Mindfulness offers tools to manage these feelings, helping you to cope with stress in a healthy way.

Scenario: The Breaking Point

Let's say it's been one of those days. You've been rushing from one task to the next, balancing work deadlines, household chores, and caring for your children. By the time evening comes, you're completely drained. Your toddler, Mia, is refusing to go to bed, and after the tenth time of getting her back into bed, you feel yourself reaching your breaking point. The frustration bubbles up, and you're on the verge of snapping.

Mindful Response:

1. **Recognize Your Stress:** The first step is acknowledging that you're feeling overwhelmed. It's okay to admit that you're not at your best right now. This recognition is the key to shifting your response.
2. **Take a Break:** If possible, step away for a few minutes. Ensure Mia is safe, and then take a short break. This might mean stepping outside for some fresh air, splashing cold water on your face, or simply sitting down and taking a few deep breaths. Allow yourself a moment to reset.
3. **Practice Self-Compassion:** Place your hand on your heart and silently say, "This is really hard right now, and it's okay to feel this way. I'm doing the best I can." Treat yourself with the same kindness and understanding you would offer a friend in a similar situation.
4. **Focus on the Present Moment:** Bring your attention back to the present. What is one small thing you can do right now to move forward? This might be as simple as gently

guiding Mia back to bed one more time or sitting with her quietly until she falls asleep.

5. **Reflect and Recharge:** Once Mia is asleep, take time to reflect on the day. What were your triggers? What can you do differently tomorrow? End your day with a small act of self-care—reading, journaling, or even just enjoying a quiet moment before bed. Remember, tomorrow is a new day, and each moment is an opportunity to begin again.

3. Dealing with Sibling Rivalry

Sibling rivalry is a common challenge in families with more than one child. Arguments, jealousy, and competition can disrupt the peace at home and leave parents feeling frustrated and unsure of how to mediate. Mindful parenting provides a way to navigate these conflicts with empathy and fairness.

Scenario: The Battle Over Toys

Imagine a scene in your living room. Your two children, eight-year-old Liam and five-year-old Sophie, are playing with a set of building blocks. Everything is going well until Liam decides he wants the block Sophie is using. Sophie refuses to give it up, and within seconds, the peaceful play turns into a heated argument. Liam grabs the block from Sophie, who retaliates by knocking over Liam's tower. Both children are now shouting, and the tension is rising.

Mindful Response:

1. **Intervene with Calmness:** Approach the situation calmly, without immediately taking sides. Sit down with both

children and take a few deep breaths together to help everyone settle.

2. **Acknowledge Both Perspectives:** Speak to each child in turn, acknowledging their feelings and perspectives. "Liam, I can see that you really wanted that block to finish your tower. Sophie, I understand that you were using it and didn't want to give it up."

3. **Encourage Problem-Solving:** Ask both children how they think the situation could be resolved. "What do you think we could do to make sure everyone gets a turn?" Guide them towards a solution, such as taking turns, sharing, or finding another block.

4. **Model Empathy:** Help them see each other's feelings. "Liam, how do you think Sophie felt when you took the block from her? Sophie, how did Liam feel when you knocked over his tower?" Encouraging them to consider each other's emotions fosters empathy and understanding.

5. **Reinforce Positive Behavior:** Once a solution is found, praise the children for their cooperation. "I'm really proud of both of you for working together to solve this problem. That's what teamwork looks like." Positive reinforcement encourages them to handle conflicts more constructively in the future.

4. Navigating Family Crises

Sometimes, families face situations that are far more difficult than the everyday challenges of parenting—such as illness, loss, financial difficulties, or major life changes. During these times, mindfulness can provide a much-needed anchor, helping both you and your children navigate the uncertainty with resilience and grace.

Scenario: Coping with Loss

Let's consider a family going through the loss of a beloved grandparent. The grief is palpable, and everyone in the family is struggling to come to terms with the loss. Your six-year-old daughter, Emma, doesn't fully understand what has happened, but she feels the sadness and confusion in the house. She starts acting out—throwing tantrums, refusing to go to school, and becoming unusually clingy.

Mindful Response:

1. **Create a Safe Space for Emotions:** Acknowledge that this is a difficult time for everyone, including your child. Let Emma know that it's okay to feel sad, confused, or even angry. Create a space where she can express her feelings freely—whether through talking, drawing, or simply sitting together in silence.

2. **Explain the Situation Honestly and Gently:** Depending on your child's age, explain the situation in a way that they can understand. Use simple, clear language. "Grandma has passed away, which means we won't see her anymore, but we will always have our memories of her. It's okay to feel sad, and it's okay to talk about how you're feeling."

3. **Model Emotional Resilience:** Allow your child to see your emotions, but also show them how you manage those emotions. It's okay to cry in front of Emma, but also let her see you finding ways to cope—whether it's through talking to others, practicing mindfulness, or remembering the good times.

4. **Maintain Routines:** In times of crisis, routines provide a sense of normalcy and security. Keep Emma's daily routine as consistent as possible, while also being flexible and understanding if she needs extra comfort or support.

5. **Seek Support:** Recognize that you don't have to navigate this alone. Reach out to family, friends, or a counselor for support. Encourage Emma to talk to a trusted adult or counselor as well, if needed. Sometimes, just knowing that there are people who care can make a big difference.

6. **Focus on Healing Together:** Over time, focus on healing as a family. Share stories, look at pictures, and remember the good times you had with your loved one. Engage in activities that bring comfort and joy, helping everyone in the family find their way through the grief together.

Conclusion: Embracing the Journey of Mindful Parenting in All Circumstances

Mindful parenting is not just for the easy days. It's for the tough days, the chaotic days, and the days when everything seems to be going wrong. It's about showing up with compassion, patience, and presence, even when it feels like the last thing you can manage. It's about understanding that every challenge is an opportunity to deepen your connection with your child, to grow as a parent, and to model resilience and grace.

As you continue on this journey, remember that it's okay to stumble. It's okay to feel overwhelmed, to make mistakes, and to have moments of doubt. What matters is how you respond—how you pick yourself up, take a deep breath, and try again. Each moment is a new opportunity to practice mindfulness, to connect with your child, and to be the kind of parent you aspire to be.

Thank you for allowing this book to be part of your parenting journey. May it serve as a source of support, inspiration, and guidance as you navigate the beautiful, complex, and rewarding path of mindful parenting. In every moment, may you find the strength to be present, the courage to be compassionate, and the wisdom to embrace each day with an open heart.

Epilogue: The Lifelong Impact of Mindful Parenting

As you reach the end of this book, it's important to recognize that the journey of mindful parenting doesn't have an endpoint. It's a lifelong process of learning, growing, and evolving alongside your child. The seeds of mindfulness that you plant today will continue to grow and bear fruit throughout your life and the lives of your children.

The Legacy of Mindfulness

Mindful parenting is more than just a set of practices or techniques; it's a way of being. It's about embodying the values of presence, compassion, and empathy in your daily interactions with your children and, by extension, with everyone you encounter. These values, when consistently modeled, become part of your family's legacy—a gift that you pass down to your children, who in turn will carry these lessons into their own lives and relationships.

Scenario: A Lifetime of Connection

Imagine yourself many years from now, sitting in a sunlit room with your grown child. You've both come a long way from the days of tantrums, bedtime stories, and family dinners. Your child is now an adult, perhaps with children of their own. As you reminisce about the years gone by, you realize that the bond you share is not just the result of being family—it's the result of the countless moments of mindful connection you cultivated over the years.

Your child shares how the lessons of mindfulness have influenced their own life—how they approach challenges with calm, how they communicate with empathy, and how they've learned to care for themselves and others with compassion. They tell you how the moments of presence, patience, and love you offered them as a child have shaped who they are today.

In that moment, you see the ripple effect of your mindful parenting. The practices you integrated into your daily life have created a foundation of trust, resilience, and love that has endured through the years. This is the legacy of mindfulness—a legacy that will continue to influence your family for generations to come.

Continuing the Journey

While this book may be coming to a close, your journey is far from over. There will always be new challenges to face, new lessons to learn, and new opportunities to grow. As your child grows, their needs and behaviors will change, and your approach to mindfulness will need to evolve as well. The key is to remain open, flexible, and committed to the values of mindfulness, no matter what life brings your way.

Tips for Continuing Your Mindful Parenting Practice:

1. **Stay Curious:** As your child grows, remain curious about their thoughts, feelings, and experiences. Ask open-ended questions, listen without judgment, and continue to

explore the world together with a sense of wonder and openness.

2. **Practice Mindfulness Together:** As your child becomes more independent, find ways to practice mindfulness together. This could be through shared meditation, mindful walks, or simply sitting quietly together at the end of a busy day.

3. **Model Lifelong Learning:** Show your child that mindfulness is a lifelong journey by continuing to learn and grow yourself. Read books, attend workshops, or explore new mindfulness practices. Share what you learn with your child, and let them see that you, too, are always growing.

4. **Cultivate Gratitude:** Make gratitude a regular part of your family's life. Whether it's through a daily gratitude practice, a gratitude jar, or simply expressing thanks to each other, this practice will help your family stay grounded in appreciation and joy.

5. **Embrace Change:** Life is full of changes, and as your child grows, your relationship will change too. Embrace these changes with grace, understanding that each stage of life brings new opportunities for connection and growth.

A Final Reflection

As you close this book, take a moment to reflect on your journey so far. What have you learned about yourself as a parent? What new insights have you gained about your child? What small changes have you already noticed in your relationship?

Remember that mindfulness is not about perfection. It's about progress, about making small, intentional choices each day that bring you closer to the parent you want to be. It's about being present for the moments that matter, even when they're messy, challenging, or imperfect.

Thank you for allowing me to be a part of your journey. I hope this book has provided you with the tools, insights, and inspiration you need to continue cultivating mindfulness in your parenting and in your life. As you move forward, may you find joy in the present moment, strength in the face of challenges, and deep, lasting connections with your child and those you love.

May your journey of mindful parenting bring you and your family peace, happiness, and a lifetime of meaningful memories.

Acknowledgments

Writing this book has been a journey of its own—a journey made possible by the support, wisdom, and inspiration of many people. I am deeply grateful to the parents who shared their stories, challenges, and triumphs with me. Your experiences have enriched this book in ways that words cannot fully express.

To my own family, thank you for your patience, love, and encouragement. Your presence in my life is the greatest gift, and it is because of you that I have learned the true meaning of mindfulness and compassion.

To the readers of this book, thank you for choosing to embark on this journey of mindful parenting. Your commitment to nurturing your children with presence and love is an inspiration, and I am honored to be a part of your parenting journey.

Finally, thank you to all those who have contributed to the field of mindfulness and parenting. Your research, teachings, and writings have paved the way for a new generation of parents who are striving to raise their children with kindness, empathy, and awareness.

May this book serve as a source of guidance and support as you continue on your path of mindful parenting.

Appendix II: Frequently Asked Questions (FAQs) About Mindful Parenting

As you navigate the journey of mindful parenting, you might encounter some common questions and challenges. This appendix is designed to address those questions, providing practical advice and insights to help you deepen your understanding and practice of mindfulness in your daily parenting life.

1. What if I don't have time for mindfulness?

One of the most common concerns parents have is finding the time to practice mindfulness amidst their busy schedules. It's important to remember that mindfulness doesn't require large blocks of time or formal meditation sessions. It's about being present in the moments you already have.

Tips:

- **Start Small:** Begin with just a few minutes of mindful breathing each day. You can do this while brushing your teeth, waiting in line, or even while your child is napping.
- **Incorporate Mindfulness into Routine Activities:** Practice mindfulness while doing daily tasks like washing dishes, folding laundry, or driving. Focus on the sensations, sounds, and movements involved in the task.
- **Mindful Moments:** Use transitions throughout the day—like getting in and out of the car, or before entering a room—as a reminder to take a deep breath and ground yourself in the present moment.

2. How do I introduce mindfulness to my child?

Introducing mindfulness to children can be simple and fun. The key is to approach it in a way that is age-appropriate and engaging.

Tips:

- **Make It Fun:** Use games and activities to teach mindfulness. For example, you can play a "mindful listening" game where you sit quietly and see how many different sounds you can notice.
- **Lead by Example:** Children learn by watching their parents. Practice mindfulness yourself, and let your child see you taking deep breaths, pausing before reacting, or spending a few quiet moments in reflection.
- **Storytelling:** Use stories and books that incorporate mindfulness themes. For younger children, you can use picture books that explore emotions, breathing, and being present.
- **Create a Routine:** Incorporate a short mindfulness practice into your child's daily routine, such as a breathing exercise before bed or a gratitude practice at dinner.

3. How can I stay mindful when I'm feeling overwhelmed?

Parenting can be overwhelming, and in those moments, staying mindful can be a challenge. It's important to acknowledge your feelings and find ways to reset.

Tips:

- **Acknowledge Your Feelings:** It's okay to feel overwhelmed. Acknowledge your emotions without judgment, and remind yourself that it's natural to feel this way sometimes.

- **Pause and Breathe:** When you notice yourself becoming overwhelmed, take a moment to pause and take a few deep breaths. This can help calm your nervous system and give you space to choose a mindful response.
- **Ground Yourself:** Focus on the physical sensations in your body—your feet on the ground, the texture of an object in your hand, or the sound of your breath. This can help bring you back to the present moment.
- **Practice Self-Compassion:** Be kind to yourself. Recognize that you're doing your best, and that it's okay to ask for help or take a break when you need it.

4. What should I do if my child resists mindfulness practices?

It's not uncommon for children to be hesitant or resistant to new practices, including mindfulness. The key is to approach it with patience, flexibility, and creativity.

Tips:

- **Be Patient:** Understand that mindfulness is a new skill, and like any skill, it takes time to develop. Be patient with your child and with yourself.
- **Adapt to Your Child's Interests:** If your child loves to move, try incorporating mindfulness into physical activities, like mindful walking or yoga. If they enjoy art, try mindful drawing or coloring.
- **Make It a Shared Activity:** Practice mindfulness together. This not only models the practice for your child but also turns it into a bonding activity.

- **Don't Force It:** If your child is particularly resistant, don't force mindfulness practices. Instead, find small ways to incorporate mindfulness into daily life, and let your child come to it in their own time.

5. How do I handle setbacks in my mindful parenting practice?

Setbacks are a normal part of any practice, including mindful parenting. What matters is how you respond to those setbacks and how you choose to move forward.

Tips:

- **Reflect on the Experience:** When you experience a setback, take some time to reflect on what happened. What triggered the setback? How did you respond? What can you learn from the experience?
- **Practice Self-Compassion:** Be gentle with yourself. Recognize that setbacks are part of the learning process, and that each one is an opportunity to grow.
- **Recommit to Your Practice:** After a setback, take a moment to recommit to your mindful parenting practice. Set an intention for how you want to move forward, and take small steps to get back on track.
- **Seek Support:** If you're struggling with setbacks, reach out for support. Talk to a friend, join a parenting group, or seek guidance from a mindfulness teacher or counselor.

6. Can mindfulness really make a difference in my parenting?

Yes, mindfulness can have a profound impact on your parenting, your relationship with your child, and your overall well-being. The benefits of mindfulness are supported by research and by the experiences of countless parents.

Benefits of Mindful Parenting:

- **Improved Emotional Regulation:** Mindfulness helps you manage your emotions more effectively, leading to fewer outbursts and more thoughtful responses to challenging situations.
- **Stronger Connection with Your Child:** Mindfulness fosters deeper connection by helping you be more present, listen more fully, and respond with empathy.
- **Reduced Stress:** Practicing mindfulness can reduce stress and increase your overall sense of well-being, making you more resilient to the demands of parenting.
- **Positive Role Modeling:** By practicing mindfulness, you model healthy ways of managing stress and emotions for your child, teaching them valuable life skills.

7. How do I maintain mindfulness as my child grows older?

As your child grows, their needs and behaviors will change, and your approach to mindful parenting will need to evolve as well. The principles of mindfulness—presence, empathy, and compassion—remain the same, but the way you apply them may shift.

Tips:

- **Adapt Your Practices:** As your child becomes more independent, you may need to find new ways to connect and practice mindfulness together. This might include more conversations about emotions, practicing mindfulness in shared activities, or encouraging your child to develop their own mindfulness practice.

- **Focus on Communication:** As children grow, communication becomes increasingly important. Use mindfulness to enhance your listening skills, and to respond to your child with understanding and empathy.
- **Encourage Autonomy:** Mindfulness can support your child's growing independence by helping them develop self-awareness, emotional regulation, and decision-making skills.
- **Stay Open to Change:** Be open to the changes that come with each stage of your child's development. Mindfulness can help you navigate these changes with flexibility and grace.

8. How can I balance mindfulness with other parenting approaches?

Mindful parenting can be integrated with a variety of other parenting approaches. The key is to find what works best for you and your family, and to use mindfulness as a foundation for your parenting choices.

Tips:

- **Combine with Positive Discipline:** Mindfulness and positive discipline work well together, as both focus on understanding and responding to your child's needs with empathy and respect.
- **Use Mindfulness as a Foundation:** Whatever parenting approach you choose, mindfulness can serve as a foundation. It helps you stay present, respond

thoughtfully, and maintain a strong connection with your child.

- **Be Flexible:** There is no one-size-fits-all approach to parenting. Be open to trying different strategies and adapting them to your family's needs, using mindfulness as a guide.

9. How can I involve my partner or co-parent in mindful parenting?

Involving your partner or co-parent in mindful parenting can strengthen your family's practice and create a more cohesive approach to raising your child.

Tips:

- **Share Your Experience:** Talk to your partner about your mindfulness practice and how it's impacting your parenting. Share what you've learned and the benefits you've noticed.
- **Practice Together:** Find ways to practice mindfulness together, whether it's through shared activities with your child, co-parenting discussions, or practicing mindfulness as a couple.
- **Encourage Open Communication:** Use mindfulness to enhance communication between you and your partner. Listen to each other's perspectives and work together to find mindful solutions to parenting challenges.
- **Support Each Other:** Recognize that each of you may have different strengths and challenges in parenting. Use mindfulness to support each other's growth and to create a united approach to mindful parenting.

10. What if mindfulness doesn't seem to be working for me?

If you're finding it difficult to practice mindfulness or you're not seeing the results you hoped for, it's important to explore why that might be. Mindfulness is a skill that takes time to develop, and it's okay to face challenges along the way.

Tips:

- **Reflect on Your Practice:** Take some time to reflect on your mindfulness practice. Are there specific areas where you're struggling? Are your expectations realistic? What changes could you make to your approach?
- **Start Small:** If mindfulness feels overwhelming, start with small, manageable practices. Even a few minutes of mindful breathing or a short pause before responding can make a difference.
- **Seek Support:** If you're struggling, don't hesitate to seek support. This could be from a mindfulness teacher, a therapist, or a supportive community of parents.
- **Be Patient:** Mindfulness is a journey, not a destination. It's normal to experience ups and downs along the way. Be patient with yourself, and remember that every moment is an opportunity to start anew.

Final Words

Mindful parenting is a lifelong journey that evolves with you and your child. It's a practice that offers countless rewards—deeper connections, greater emotional resilience, and a more peaceful, fulfilling family life. As you continue on this path, remember that mindfulness is not about being perfect. It's about showing up, being present, and practicing compassion, both for yourself and for your child.

Each step you take, no matter how small, brings you closer to the parent you aspire to be. May this book serve as a source of guidance, inspiration, and support as you navigate the beautiful, challenging, and rewarding journey of mindful parenting.

Thank you for being a part of this journey. May you continue to grow, learn, and find joy in the moments of connection, presence, and love that mindful parenting brings into your life.

Final Reflection: Your Journey Forward

As you close this book and step forward into the ongoing journey of mindful parenting, it's important to recognize that this journey is deeply personal and ever-evolving. The principles and practices outlined in these pages are meant to serve as guideposts, not rigid rules. Mindful parenting is about tuning into the unique dynamics of your family, embracing the messy and beautiful moments alike, and continuously adapting your approach to meet the changing needs of your child and yourself.

1. The Ongoing Practice of Presence

Mindfulness is a practice that deepens with time and consistency. The more you practice being present with your child, the more natural it will become. It's in those quiet, ordinary moments—like sharing a meal, walking together, or sitting side by side—that the true essence of mindful parenting is cultivated. These moments of presence, when you are fully engaged and connected, are the heartbeats of a strong, nurturing relationship.

Scenario: Finding Presence in the Everyday

Imagine a typical weekday evening. You've just finished dinner, and the house is buzzing with post-dinner activities. Dishes need to be done, homework needs to be checked, and bedtime routines are looming. But instead of rushing through these tasks, you decide to slow down. You take a moment to sit with your child as they work on a school project, offering your full attention. You notice the way their brow furrows in concentration, the way they explain their ideas with enthusiasm, and the way they light up when you show genuine interest. In this moment, everything else fades into the background, and you are fully present with your child. This is mindful parenting in action—a simple, yet profound commitment to being there, fully and completely, in the everyday moments.

2. Embracing Imperfection

One of the most freeing aspects of mindful parenting is the acceptance of imperfection. Parenting is not about doing everything right—it's about showing up, even when things are messy or complicated. It's about recognizing that mistakes and missteps are part of the process, and that each challenge is an opportunity to learn and grow.

Scenario: Embracing the Mess

Consider a morning when everything seems to go wrong. The alarm didn't go off, breakfast was a chaotic rush, and your child had a meltdown over a forgotten homework assignment. In the past, you might have felt frustrated or guilty, questioning your ability to manage it all. But through the lens of mindfulness, you see this morning differently. You recognize the chaos as a natural part of life, and instead of dwelling on what went wrong, you focus on how you handled it—how you took a breath, stayed as calm as possible, and found a way to move forward. You remind yourself that it's okay to have messy mornings, and that what matters most is the love and effort you bring to each day.

3. The Power of Self-Reflection

Self-reflection is a cornerstone of mindful parenting. It allows you to step back, observe your thoughts, feelings, and behaviors, and make conscious choices about how you want to respond. Regular self-reflection helps you stay aligned with your values, recognize areas for growth, and celebrate the progress you've made.

Exercise: A Self-Reflection Ritual

Set aside a few minutes at the end of each day for self-reflection. Find a quiet space, take a few deep breaths, and ask yourself the following questions:

- What went well today? Where did I feel most connected with my child?
- Were there moments when I felt disconnected or reactive? What triggered those feelings?

- How did I handle challenges today? What could I do differently next time?
- What am I grateful for in my relationship with my child?

By regularly engaging in this practice, you cultivate a deeper awareness of your parenting journey and foster continuous growth.

4. Building a Supportive Community

Mindful parenting is a journey best taken with the support of others. Whether it's through connecting with other parents, joining a mindfulness group, or seeking guidance from a mentor or therapist, building a supportive community can make a significant difference in your practice. Sharing your experiences, challenges, and successes with others not only provides valuable insights but also reinforces the understanding that you are not alone on this journey.

Scenario: The Strength of Community

Imagine joining a local mindfulness group that meets once a month. At each meeting, parents share their experiences, discuss challenges, and offer support to one another. One month, you share a particularly difficult situation you faced with your child—a time when you struggled to stay mindful and ended up reacting out of frustration. As you speak, the group listens with empathy, and several parents share similar experiences. Together, you explore ways to approach such situations differently, and you leave the meeting feeling understood, supported, and inspired to continue your practice. This sense of community strengthens your resolve and reminds you that mindful parenting is a shared journey.

5. Passing Mindfulness to the Next Generation

One of the most powerful aspects of mindful parenting is the legacy it creates. By practicing mindfulness, you're not only enhancing your own life and your relationship with your child—you're also passing on valuable life skills that your child will carry into their own adulthood. The mindfulness you model and teach today will influence how your child navigates their own challenges, relationships, and self-awareness in the future.

Scenario: A Legacy of Mindfulness

Years from now, your child might reflect on their own childhood and the lessons they learned from you. They might remember the way you always took a deep breath before responding in difficult situations, or how you helped them calm down with mindful breathing when they were upset. As an adult, they might find themselves using those same techniques in their own life—whether it's managing stress at work, communicating in a relationship, or parenting their own children. In this way, the mindfulness you practice today becomes a lasting legacy, shaping not only your child's future but also the future of the generations to come.

A Final Word: Trusting Your Path

Mindful parenting is a deeply personal and evolving journey. There will be days when you feel like you've got it all together, and other days when everything seems to fall apart. Through it all, remember to trust your path. Trust that the love, presence, and intention you bring to your parenting are enough. Trust that each step you take—no matter how small—moves you and your child closer to a life filled with connection, peace, and joy.

As you move forward, may you continue to find inspiration in the practice of mindfulness. May you embrace the ups and downs of parenting with grace and resilience. And may you always remember that the heart of mindful parenting is love—love for your child, love for yourself, and love for the journey you are on together.

Thank you for being a part of this journey. May your path be filled with mindfulness, compassion, and endless moments of connection.

Book Summary/Blurb:

"Mindful Parenting 101: The Art of Presence in Parenthood" is more than a guide—it's a lifeline for parents navigating the complexities of raising children while facing life's toughest challenges. Co-authored by Jawahar Soundararajan and Karthik Raghuraman, two fathers who turned their battles with serious illness into a transformative approach to parenting, this book offers insights and strategies to help you cultivate mindfulness, resilience, and emotional connection with your children. Discover how the practice of being fully present can enrich your parenting journey, even in the face of adversity."

Author Bios:

Jawahar Soundararajan is a software architect based in Michigan, where he lives with his wife and two daughters. After overcoming lymphoma twice, Jawahar embraced mindfulness as a way to cherish every moment with his family. His journey has inspired him to share the profound lessons of presence and intention in parenting.

Karthik Raghuraman is a Digital Learning Lead living in New Jersey with his wife and two sons. Diagnosed with Crohn's disease in his early 30s, Karthik found strength in mindfulness, using it to prioritize emotional connection and resilience in his parenting. His story is one of perseverance and the power of mindful living.